The Power of Angels

DISCOVER HOW TO
CONNECT, COMMUNICATE,
AND HEAL WITH THE ANGELS

✷

The
Power
of Angels

✷

JOANNE BROCAS

NEW PAGE BOOKS
A division of The Career Press, Inc.
Pompton Plains, NJ

THE POWER OF ANGELS

EDITED BY JODI BRANDON

TYPESET BY EILEEN MUNSON

Cover design by Amanda Kain
Cover art by Marius Michael-George
Printed in the U.S.A.

To order this title, please call toll-free 1-800-CAREER-1 (NJ and Canada: 201-848-0310) to order using VISA or MasterCard, or for further information on books from Career Press.

The Career Press, Inc.
220 West Parkway, Unit 12
Pompton Plains, NJ 07444
www.careerpress.com
www.newpagebooks.com

Library of Congress Cataloging-in-Publication Data
Brocas, Joanne.
  The power of angels : discover how to connect, communicate, and heal with the angels / by Joanne Brocas.
      pages cm
  Includes index.
  ISBN 978-1-60163-319-4 -- ISBN 978-1-60163-467-2 (ebook) 1. Angels.
I. Title.

BL477.B755 2014
202'.15--dc23

2013046729

To my husband, Jock;

you are the light in my life.

To my grandparents Jack and Gladys Joce;

you are always in my heart.

And most of all to

God and His angels.

❈

Disclaimer

This book is not an independent guide for self-healing. The author is not a medical doctor, psychiatrist, or psychologist, and she does not diagnose diseases or prescribe treatments. No medical claims or cures are implied in this book, even if specific "benefits," "healing," or "treatments" are mentioned. Readers are advised to practice the methods in this book only under the guidance and supervision of a qualified healthcare professional and to use these methods at their own risk. The author and publisher make no claim or obligation and take no legal responsibility for the results of reading this book or of using the suggested methods; deny all liability for any injuries or damages that readers may incur; and are to be held harmless against any claim, liability, loss, or damage caused by or arising from following any suggestions made in this book.

Contents

Introduction

An angel can illumine the thought
and mind of man by strengthening the
power of vision and by bringing within
his reach some truth which the angel
himself contemplates.

—St. Thomas Aquinas

The Power of Angels will help you to form a strong and clear connection to the angels and to your very own guardian angel. You will also be introduced to *Heaven's Mighty Seven*—the Archangels—and discover how their unique powers can help you to heal, improve, and empower the circumstances of your health and your life. There are many angels surrounding you, just waiting for the opportunity to connect with you. Following the step-by-step guidance and using the practical exercises and energy techniques outlined within this book will help you to activate "angel power" within your life.

You will discover more about the angels in general, along with the array of signs they leave for you to help alert you to their presence. Signs often include angel nudges and messages, which are subtle intuitive insights that are given to help guide you in the best direction along your life's path. Signs, nudges, and subtle messages are the beginning stages of angelic communication itself, so it is wise to learn and decipher the language of the angels in this way to help you begin your initial connection with them.

God created angels for the purpose of helping, healing, serving, and protecting humankind. Angels are God's holy messengers who take our prayers to God, and also deliver God's answers and blessings to us in ways that will always be for our greatest good. God has even assigned you your very own guardian angel to help watch over you during your entire lifetime. There is nothing that will ever be of too much trouble for the angelic kingdom to be of service to you. The power of God's angels can help your life improve in many ways when you learn to rely on a source of power that is greater than you alone.

The Power of Angels will teach you how to spiritually see, hear, and sense the angels around you.

To be able to do this, you first need to heal any accumulated negative energies that you may have stored within you, known as energetic stress, as this can impede clear communication. An overload of energetic stress held within your individual energy vibration, otherwise known as your aura, will cause static on the energy link held between you and the angels, interfering with your connection. This type of energetic stress will make your connection fuzzy, and it will then be difficult to interpret what you receive. Just think of a radio station or television channel that isn't tuned in properly and you will get an idea of the interference energetic stress causes. This book will offer the solutions you need to help you heal and clear the energetic stress within your aura so that you can begin to prepare the optimum energetic frequency required for a clear connection to the angels and for angelic communication to take place.

I have been in touch with the spirit world ever since I was a small child, and I have kept a strong and natural connection to my guardian angel throughout my life. My guardian angel has encouraged me when I needed it, sent me healing energy when I have been ill or hurt (especially when I broke my leg just before I got married), saved me from harm on several occasions, given me insight through my dreams and meditations, and continually guided me throughout my spiritual development and life. Because I have kept the connection to my guardian angel clear and strong, I have developed a deep level of insight and experience that I can now use to help you establish your own natural connection with your guardian angel and other angelic beings. This book was written just for you.

Each chapter of this book will help you to develop the spiritual insight to decipher and discern exactly what it is the angels wish to impart. Overall, *The Power of Angels* will help you to develop your relationship with a higher power. Angels are a stepping stone toward forming a personal relationship with God. God's holy angels can and will help you in all your ways!

> For He shall give His angels charge over you, to keep you in all your ways.
>
> —Psalm 91:11 (New King James Version)

Chapter 1
Angels Exist

Then he dreamed, and behold, a ladder
was set up on the earth, and its top
reached to heaven; and there the angels
of God were ascending and descending
on it.

—Genesis 28:12
(New King James Version)

Millions of people around the world have a fas-
cination with angels and believe that they are real.
Many of these same people have had their own personal encounters with angelic beings, and their lives
have been positively changed because of this. Angels
exist among us and they carry out God's will to help
serve humanity for our greatest good. We have our
very own guardian angel, who will stay with us

throughout our entire lifetime, and we also have access to a host of heavenly angels and the mighty and powerful Archangels.

Angels will help us whenever we reach out to a higher power and ask for spiritual assistance. We are never alone, as we have many unseen spiritual friends who walk with us along our life's path; all we need to do is learn how to listen to the helpful guidance they offer. Young children quite naturally listen to the voices of their guardian angels because they are still pure of heart. They haven't yet begun to form any unhealthy beliefs or limiting thoughts (unlike most adults) that would interfere with their spiritual connection. They are also still very closely connected to the spirit world and to their guardian angels, who are assigned to watch over them as they learn to adapt to their new physical lives and families.

Young children also find it easier to live fully within the present moment, not going over the past and not concerning themselves about the future. They are non-judgmental, and they have a special magical quality and innocence about them that allows their aura to hold a lot of spiritual light; this is what activates a powerful and natural connection to the angels. Imagination and creativity also help to activate a natural connection to the angelic realm, and children love to imagine and create things. Many young children have an imaginary friend, who is often a child's guardian angel appearing to the child as a spirit child to help the child settle into his or her physical existence. Children often lose their natural connection to their guardian angel when they become more focused on physical life. This does not mean that their angel has left them, though, as their guardian angel will stay by their side throughout their entire lifetime, continuing to whisper helpful guidance.

Most adults have allowed their sensitivity to close down due to numerous things, such as loss of faith and belief in a higher power to help them (usually due to life's adversities and struggles causing a disbelief in God). Overwhelming stress from the daily pressures of life (money, family, work, home) also assist in numbing our senses to the helpful guidance of our guardian angel. Physical exhaustion from not getting enough rest; physical illness and pain; depression and emotional pain; unhealthy habits, addictions, a negative mind-set, blocked creativity, limiting beliefs, and fear; and destructive emotions such as greed, jealousy, envy, anger, hatred, and un-forgiveness—all are very big culprits in helping to diminish our awareness and natural sensitivity to our guardian angel.

Guardian angels love to whisper their helpful guidance and encouragement to us within our daily lives so that we can begin to make the positive changes we need to make for our greatest good. Often, though, as previously mentioned, this angelic guidance goes unheard, especially when a person is overly stressed or has lost faith and hope. If someone is particularly materialistic, which simply means that he or she has placed more focus on the temporary pleasures of the material world instead of on spiritual growth and transformation, then he will also close off his heart and mind to the influence of his guardian angels.

Every soul has at least one guardian angel assigned to him or her; some people will have several. Our guardian angels will never leave us, and they will continue to whisper their helpful guidance to us throughout our lifetime in the hope that, one day, we will eventually begin to listen. This book will help you begin to listen to the wise and wonderful voice of your guardian angel or angels, for in choosing it, you have already begun. Let's start by first exploring the angelic hierarchy!

The Celestial Hierarchy

The most famous research regarding the celestial hierarchy came from the scholar Dionysius the

Areopagite, who wrote a book called *The Celestial Hierarchy* during the fourth or fifth century. From his research, there are nine angelic choirs, which are also divided into three separate orders or triads — the higher, middle, and lower levels of angels. Each angelic choir has separate duties and Divine attributes that they use to serve the will of God, to help the universe, and to serve humankind.

The first order of angels includes those who are closest to God and who possess the deepest knowledge of God. Their work within the universe is concerned with the direct manifestations of God. The second order of angels includes those who have power over all creation and who manage the daily function of the universe. They carry out the orders of the angels above them, along with governing the angels below them according to God's will. The third order of angels includes those who are nearest to humankind and who are involved with human affairs and life on earth; they include the mighty and powerful Archangels and our very own guardian angels. The study of angels is known as *angelology*.

The First Order of Angels
1. The Seraphim.
2. The Cherubim.
3. The Thrones.

The Second Order of Angels

4. The Dominions.

5. The Virtues.

6. The Powers.

The Third Order of Angels

7. The Principalities.

8. The Archangels.

9. The Angels. (From this group we have the best-known of all the angels: the guardian angels.)

The Seraphim

The Seraphim are magnificent angels of love, light, and illumination that surround, protect, and are closest to the throne of God. They are depicted as fiery spirits, "glowing ones" or "burning ones," as the light they shine is so intensely bright that it looks just like burning flames. They are the highest choir of angels and are therefore superior to all of the other angels ranked below them within the celestial hierarchy. The Seraphim hold a very elevated and enlightened vibration because they are so close to God. They shine brightly with their love, glory, and constant praise for God and they also shine God's love out to all of His creation. Their angelic power can help to dispel the shadows of darkness through the purification of their intense burning flames of light energy.

In the Old Testament, the Seraphim are mentioned by Isaiah as each having six wings; two wings are used to fly, two are used to cover their face, and two are used to cover their feet. In art, they are usually painted with red and gold wings to represent the flames and heat of intense fiery light. It is said that they fly above the throne of God, and their Divine role is to constantly sing the praises of God; they sing "Holy, Holy, Holy" and in doing so, they also maintain the vibration of creation.

The Cherubim

The Cherubim are ranked the second highest in the nine choirs of angels. They are powerful guardians of the Divine throne and are personal attendants of God. One of their main responsibilities is to magnify the glory, power, and will of God. They are keepers of celestial records, of the stars and the heavens. The Cherubim possess a deep knowledge and insight about the mysteries of heaven and knowledge of God, and being enlightened, they help to bestow this wisdom to the angels of the ranks below them.

They have a likeness to man (their figure and hands) and are depicted with four faces—that of a man, lion, ox, and eagle appearing on each side of the head, which means that they can travel in any direction without having to take their eyes off the throne of God. They also have four wings: two reaching upward toward the Divine throne, and the other two for covering their body. The Cherubim are mentioned in the Bible as guarding the entrance to the Garden of Eden and the Tree of Life. Ornamental golden cherubs can be seen standing guard at the entrances of many temples and palaces, symbolizing the energy of Divine protection. They usually appear in pairs.

The Thrones

The Thrones are the third choir of angels within the highest level of the celestial hierarchy. The Thrones are mighty angels of justice and authority who emanate the light of God because they are so closely connected to the Divine power. They carry out God's justice in accordance with God's will and are associated with the power of judgment. The Thrones also have the task of looking after the planets. Thrones are often depicted as great wheels with many eyes and glowing with light—a bizarre appearance. The Thrones are said to have been used as God's chariot, which explains the reference to wheels. The mighty Thrones are often portrayed as angels carrying the scales of justice.

The Dominions

The Dominions are the highest-ranked angels in the middle level of the celestial hierarchy; they belong to the fourth choir of angels. They are said to have power over all creation and carry out the daily functioning of the universe in alignment with God's laws. The Dominions help to regulate the duties of the lower-ranked angels and are therefore also known as *managers* of the angels. They receive orders from the higher-ranked angels and are responsible for maintaining order and balance in the universe by carrying out these orders. They are often portrayed as carrying a scepter with an orb of light, which represents authority.

The Virtues

The Virtues are the fifth choir of angels, within the middle level of the celestial hierarchy. These mighty angels are very powerful in strength and virtue. They are responsible for maintaining the natural world, and they help control the elements and weather. They have control over the seasons, the stars, the moon, the sun, and all of the planets. The powerful Virtues help to bestow God's miracles and blessings on Earth where needed.

The Powers

The Powers are the sixth choir of angels, within the middle level of the celestial hierarchy. The Powers have a big job to do, as they help to protect us from harm and keep the world in balance. The Powers help maintain peace and order in the universe according to God's will. They have one of the most dangerous tasks, as they are responsible for maintaining the border between heaven and Earth. They are spiritual warriors who make sure that the fallen angel Satan and his demons do not overthrow the Earth. They protect the celestial portals between the two realms and ensure that any newly departed souls safely reach their destination in the spiritual realms.

The Principalities

The Principalities are the seventh choir of angels, in the lowest level of the celestial hierarchy. The Principalities are protectors and guardians of the world's nations, cities, and sacred sites. They help to keep watch over the various large and important world systems (such as religions), politics, and influential world leaders, helping to ensure God's will of peace. The Principalities also help to manage the angels ranked directly below them. They are often depicted in human form wearing soldiers' clothing and sandals.

The Archangels

The mighty and powerful Archangels are the eighth choir of angels, in the lowest level of the celestial hierarchy. Archangels are known as *chief angels*, and they have important tasks and responsibilities bestowed on them by God. The most important role of the Archangels is to help carry out the will of God. They work in alignment with God's will to assist humanity and to communicate God's messages. The mighty Archangels have helped to convey God's messages to His people at critical times in history. The Archangel Gabriel announced to Mary that she was to give birth to Jesus. Because of their direct role in assisting humans, they also oversee the work of the angels and guardian angels from the lowest rank in the celestial hierarchy. Archangels are the most frequently mentioned angels in the Bible.

The best known of all the Archangels is the Archangel Michael. He is the oldest of the Archangels, who is given the role of protector and is God's warrior angel. Together with his band of angels, he helps prevent Satan and his demons (often known as dark angels) from playing havoc on Earth. Archangels can also belong to other angelic choirs, and this is when things can become confusing. For example, The Archangel Michael is also said to be a Seraphim angel; this suggests that Archangels have more power bestowed on them by God than their rank dictates. Because of their power they can help govern over the tasks of many angelic choirs.

According to the Book of Revelation, there are seven Archangels who stand in the presence of God, but only four are mentioned; they are the mighty and powerful Archangels Michael, Gabriel, Raphael, and Uriel. The identity of the other three is subject to debate. The Archangels also have unique attributes and powers associated with them that represent an aspect of God. They bring through the Divine light, which is manifested through specific rays of color into the world to help assist us. You will discover deeper insights into the power of the Archangels, their Divine roles, and their Divine rays of light in Chapter 7.

The Angels

This wonderful choir of angels ministers to us, and from this particular group we also have the best-known of all the angels: the guardian angels. *Angels* is a generic term for all of the angels in the heavenly hierarchy, but Dionysius reserves this term specifically for the lowest rank of angelic beings. Angels are Divine messengers who take our prayer requests to God to be heard, and bring back the answers in alignment with our greatest good. They act as intermediaries between God and humankind and are concerned with earthly matters, but they are not allowed to interfere with the free will of man; we must ask for their assistance. They do like to whisper their helpful guidance to us in the hope that we will listen, and they love to inspire our minds with bright new ideas.

Guardian angels are constantly with us, and they watch over us helping to guide and protect us throughout our lifetime. When our time eventually comes to cross over into the spiritual realm, it is our guardian angel who will be there to greet us, helping to guide us safely to our new dimension in our new adventure. Along with the guardian angels there are multitudes of angels that belong to the lowest choir of angels, and they are very happy to help us if we ask them for their assistance. Just as people have certain gifts and talents, so do the multitude of angels, and therefore the angels within this celestial choir can cover many unique specialties.

Angels are typically unseen spiritual beings who walk among us. They can, however, temporarily appear in human form whenever angelic intervention is needed and if it is the will of God. They also appear in the guise that most people associate with angels—a spiritual being with white feathered wings. Furthermore, angels can manifest any appearance, color, and form they choose, and they do not need wings to fly, as many people naturally assume. Now that you have been introduced to the angelic hierarchy it is time to find out more about the angels in general.

*D*ivine *Messengers*

The word *angel* is derived from the Greek word *angelos*, meaning "messenger." Whenever we pray to God, it is our guardian angels who deliver our requests to a higher power. Answers from a higher power are always given, even when we feel unheard because no physical improvement or change has manifested. Sometimes, the best help we can receive is for our prayer requests *not* to be granted. We need to trust that the angels are helping us in the best possible way. Some prayer requests can take more time to be answered; there may be other things that need to be learned, overcome, or experienced before you can receive your answer. Other times, it is for our own good that we do not get what we ask for, because it would not serve us well in the long run.

We have a limited view of what we feel is good for us compared to that of a higher power, which can clearly see the best path we need to take. Whenever you ask the angels for their help, you are also inviting God to join you in making the best decisions together. In doing so, you will find a more positive outcome is achieved than by making your own decisions and relying solely on your rational mind.

Many people worry about talking to their angels because they believe that they should send their prayer requests directly to God, and that all praise for any spiritual help should go to God. Angels do not want to be worshipped in any way, and any praise and thanks for the blessings and guidance you receive in your life should always be directed to God. Angels are created beings who are sent by God to do His will to help minister to us. Therefore, when you pray directly to God, then God will send you His angels to help you. However, God also gave you free will to ask a higher power for assistance, so whenever you ask your guardian angel for help, then you will also naturally connect to God's love because you are reaching out to God through your angel. The angels are Divine messengers, so they are very happy for you to ask them for their assistance.

"*Ask and it Is Given*"

In the Holy Bible (Matthew 7:7) we are told, "Ask and it will be given to you; seek and you will find; knock and the door will be opened to you." Whenever you go within and you ponder different things about your life, your destiny, and other questions that perplex you, then you are seeking answers from a source that is greater than yourself alone. This process of thinking will begin to activate spiritual assistance within your life to help guide you toward finding the answers that you are seeking. God has heard your internal questioning and He is now bringing you the answers that you need to help you move forward in your life; the rest is up to you. This is what it means to co-create with a higher power.

God moves, you move, and then God will move again within your life. If you don't move, what you really want is not going to get handed to you just because you asked God for it. You earn spiritual blessings and God's favor when you are willing to grow in spiritual maturity and become responsible for the way you live your life. God has a great plan for your life if you are willing to listen, and He is sending you His holy angels to help you in all your ways. Angels are innumerable (it is said that there are too many to count), so there are more than enough angels to help you; there are more than enough angels to help every single person who is alive today.

Angels are not allowed to intervene in your life without your permission. This is because God has given you free will to create your life through your own choices. You can try to do it all on your own, or you can ask for spiritual help, which will make your life a lot easier. The first stage of awakening in spiritual maturity is to know that you need to lean on a higher power to help you create a happy and fulfilling life. God has all the answers you need to help you overcome any problems, obstacles, and adversities in your life. There is nothing you cannot cope with, with God on your side, and when God is for you, there is nothing more powerful that can ever be against you.

Angels are naturally drawn to celebrations of love. They will attend marriages, engagements, births, and birthdays, and they also attend funerals. Angels will accompany the newly deceased spirit, who will usually attend his or her own funeral service, and offer healing comfort to the grieving. Angels will always congregate wherever praise and worship for their creator God are being lovingly and sincerely given. Wherever the angels have been, they will also leave us subtle signs of their presence. Angel signs are usually symbolic in nature and are twofold; they can let us know that the angels are around us, and they can also help us to gain answers and insight into what we need to know. Signs left by the angels can appear everywhere and also come in a variety of ways. Their main purpose of these angel signs is to try and reach our conscious awareness of their presence so that we can deepen our faith and belief in a higher power.

Our rational mind needs something tangible to help us connect with the angels, as most people are "seeing before believing" kinds of people. Angel signs can diminish in frequency when you no longer always need to receive them in order to believe that they have heard your request. However, there are also many people who feel that the angels are not listening to them, simply because they do not physically hear or see them. They may be waiting for a loud angelic voice to answer them, or waiting to witness an angelic being standing before them, and because of this, they will automatically block out all other avenues of contact. As spiritual beings, the angels will mainly try to reach you through supernatural means. In other words, they will work through your intuitive nature, your higher mind, and your conscience to help get your attention and to deliver insightful messages to you. Do not miss out on the loving, wise counsel of the celestial realm because you expect to have different communication results. You will find out all about angelic signs and messages in Chapter 3.

Angels are sent by God to help protect you from physical harm, guide you along the right path, and nudge you back on track whenever you deviate from your life purpose. The angel who is best able and most suitable to do this job is your very own guardian angel.

Guardian Angels

Guardian angels are assigned to each individual to guard, guide, and protect him or her until it is his or her time to cross over to the spirit world. Your guardian angel is with you from the moment you are born and will stay by your side, lovingly helping you from behind the scenes throughout your entire life. The only time that your guardian angel can intervene and help you, without your direct permission to do so, is if you are in mortal danger. This is often known as angelic intervention, and there have been many fascinating stories from around the world of mysterious strangers saving people in their hour of need only to disappear again before any thanks can be given.

Guardian angels work overtime on our behalf and often help to divert us from potential harm, all unbeknownst to us. They can do this by gently influencing us to maybe drive a different route to work, to walk a different path home, or to delay us from going somewhere planned. Angels can help to misplace items such as our car keys and our house keys, and they can even temporarily prevent our car from starting if need be, all for our greatest good. We often get angry, frustrated, and irritable when these things happen, yet our angels are still happy to help us without any gratitude on our part because we are unaware of how we are being protected. The next time you are delayed in some way and it is totally out of your control, take a moment to think whether it might be your guardian angel intervening in some way, which will always be for your greatest good, even if it doesn't seem to be that way at the time.

Your guardian angel has felt all of your emotions, both happy and sad, and is also aware of your concerns and fears, along with your hopes, desires, and dreams. Guardian angels know what your greatest potential is in this lifetime, and they want to help you reach it. They will do their best to gently influence you to go in the right direction so that you can accomplish your life's tasks and fulfill your spiritual lessons. Your guardian angel will seek to remind you to get back on track whenever you deviate from your original life plan. Guardian angels do this in numerous ways, such as intervening in your dream state to help reveal a significant message to you so that it filters through into your conscious mind. Dreams are often used to reach a person, especially when the person is mentally stressed and therefore unable to connect to his or her intuition, the avenue by which the angels most like to reach us. However, if a person goes way off his or her intended path and all else fails to reach him or her, then his guardian angel will also allow what are known as "wake-up calls" to enter the person's life, as this is what will be needed to help the person to reevaluate his or her current life direction.

These wake-up calls often include temporary struggles and difficulties that can also serve as opportunities for spiritual growth. Once you have gained what you needed to receive from the wake-up call, or once you have reevaluated the current direction of your life path, with the intention of making positive and significant change, then you will overcome your adversity and you will begin to move forward in your life, gaining in spiritual strength and achieving a new level of spiritual maturity.

Many people wonder if their guardian angel is male or female, but angels are androgynous (neither male nor female), and they do not marry or have relationships in the same way that we do. However, when you learn how to spiritually see and sense your guardian angel around you, you may find that it will appear to you as either male or female, or that you can sense a feminine energy or a masculine energy associated with it. Angels do this for our benefit and to help us connect with them in a way that we are most comfortable with.

Your guardian angel in its natural state is a glorious spirit being of high vibrational light energies that are translucent to your physical vision. To give you some idea about their natural state, just think about being outdoors on a glorious sunny day and noticing the light emanations sparkling all around you, which up close will resemble dancing dots of light. You can now imagine a beautiful angel with this magical form of dancing dots of light energies pulsating all around it. Guardian angels can sparkle with multi-colored light energies and frequencies, and you can sometimes catch a very quick glimpse of these angel sparkles with your physical vision.

Thinking about your guardian angel will begin to draw your angel close to your aura, and this will help you begin your initial connection with your guardian angel. Angels are energetic beings, just as we are (we have a spiritual anatomy as well as a physical anatomy), and energy follows thought, so when we think of our guardian angel, this mental process will help to create an energetic link directly to our guardian angel, and then our guardian angel will gladly do what it can to let us know it is close by. The most important way for you to actively begin your connection with your guardian angel is to simply ask it for its spiritual assistance.

Practical Exercise:
How to Start Your Angelic Connection

The initial way you go about asking your guardian angel for help is to simply form and hold a strong mental intention to connect with your guardian angel. Remember: energy follows thought, which creates a spiritual link directly to your guardian angel. It really is as simple and as easy as that to help you first activate the connection. Use the following three step-by-step instructions to help guide you through the quick and easy process of connecting with your guardian angel:

1. Ask.

2. Have faith and surrender.

3. Take inspired action.

Ask

Mentally send your intention to your guardian angel stating your desire to connect. Now clearly ask a question within your mind as specifically as you can, one you require some guidance or help with. Example: "Dear angel, can you please help me to find the best romantic partner for my greatest good? Thank you." (Stating "for my greatest good" will allow a higher power to override anything that is not beneficial for you.) You have now activated angel power to work for you within your life because you have reached out to a higher power for spiritual assistance, instead of trying to figure things out all on your own.

Have Faith and Surrender

This next stage will require you to leave your request in the hands of a higher power, with the faith that your request is being dealt with. Whenever you let go and surrender your request to a higher power, it is your faith that will determine how quickly you begin to draw spiritual assistance toward you to help you in your life. Developing faith in a higher power is a sign of spiritual maturity. During this waiting period you are also not meant to be concerned with the time frame of how long it will take for your specific request to be manifested/fulfilled/delivered. It may take days, weeks, months, or even years, depending on what you need to experience, learn, overcome, or fulfill. If what you asked for doesn't get delivered to you, you will soon find that there is something even greater just around the corner, which will also be more beneficial to you in the long run. You are to simply believe that your request is being dealt with and that in Divine timing you will receive Divine direction, instruction, intervention, or delivery when heaven is ready to move. Many things go on behind the scenes of your life in the spiritual realm that are unseen to you before they become part of your physical existence. Having faith during this waiting period will ensure that you keep the energetic line of connection held between you and your angel open and free of interference.

Take Inspired Action

This third and final step requires you to take inspired action if any action is needed on your part to help you receive your specific request. This is the power of co-creating. Let's go back to the example of asking your guardian angel for help to find you romantic love. It has been several months now since your request and you have not yet met anyone, but even so, you have kept the lines of connection to your guardian angel open through the faith you have that this will eventually happen. One day, you feel the intuitive pull to visit a new coffee shop for lunch in a completely different area of town, and you decide to go. While there, you bump into an old friend who is with his or her friend, who is also single and looking for love. You both feel a spark of chemistry ignite between you, and so it begins! All of this happened in this way because your guardian angel began whispering its helpful guidance to you, positively influencing you to cross paths with your old friend.

What to Ask Your Guardian Angel

You can ask your guardian angel to help you with any request you may have. You are not wasting your guardian angel's time when you ask for assistance, as guardian angels are always happy to help you. Try to be as specific as possible in your requests and simply address them to "angel" or "guardian angel." Here are several examples of what you can ask your guardian angel to help you with.

Dear guardian angel:

* Please can you help me find a peaceful solution to a problem that is currently ongoing?

* Please can you help me with the process of forgiveness?

* Please can you help me forgive myself?

* Please can you send me healing energy for (be specific)?

* Please can you help me overcome my weakness with (be specific)?

* Please can you help me create more abundance in my life?

* Please can you help me find romantic love or friendship?

* Please can you help inspire me with new creative ideas?

* Please can you help me in the development of my creative gifts and talents?

* Please can you help protect me during my journey?

* Please can you help me with my spiritual growth and development?

* Please can you help me to find my lost object? (Be specific.)

* Please can you help me find a parking space?

Now that you have received several examples of what to ask your guardian angel, you can begin to ask your own unique questions. Sometimes we don't receive simply because we don't ask.

Important Warning

Never ever ask the angels to help you hurt or harm another person. They will never do that, as they are unconditionally loving spiritual beings in alignment with the will of God. In doing so, you will also incur karma. Karma can be incurred with your intentions as well as with your actions. What you think, feel, and do generates a specific vibration in your aura. The quality of energy that you give out, you will also attract back to you — or, as the following sayings go, "what goes around, comes around"; "like attracts like"; and "cause and effect." Negative thoughts, vengeful thoughts, hateful thoughts, angry thoughts, and judgmental thoughts will all help to interfere with the quality of your energy vibration, and they will drain and weaken your energy frequency, limiting your aura power. A drained and weakened energy frequency will interfere with your angelic connection, it will also interfere with your physical health, and it will certainly interfere with your ability to co-create your dreams and desires, because you will lack the aura power you need to make them happen. It does not serve you to hold any negativity within you because if you do you are simply attacking your own power to be successful, healthy, and happy.

Angels do not take sides and they will work in alignment with your greatest good and for the good of all to help bring peace and harmony. If you are looking for justice, you need to leave this in the hands of God to deal with. If you have an ongoing dispute with someone, your guardian angel can interact with the other person's guardian angel to try to find a suitable and peaceful solution that can be of benefit to all involved. Of course, free will is still honored, and oftentimes someone's anger, stubbornness, or the need to be right or more powerful will counteract and override any good influence given to him by his guardian angel.

When Requests Are Not Answered

There are four main reasons why our requests do not get answered or receive immediate angelic assistance:

1. **Pre-chosen spiritual lessons and certain life experiences:** This is for the purpose of helping our soul to progress and to achieve what we set out to achieve.

2. **Karma:** The quality of energy that we give out we will also attract back to us. It is our responsibility to develop our spiritual maturity so that we can live in alignment with God's laws of Divine truth and Divine love. In other words, to live in the light, so that you will create more light, add more light to the world, and attract more light.

3. **Not in alignment with God's will and for our greatest good:** What we have asked for simply does not agree with God's will for our lives and does not serve our greatest good in the long run.

4. **We are not ready:** We are simply not ready to receive what it is we want because we have more preparation work to do beforehand. We may need to develop our gifts and talents, to increase our knowledge and wisdom, to attain a higher level of spiritual growth, or to experience certain life lessons.

To finish this chapter I will leave you with a powerful angel affirmation that you can say whenever you feel the need for protection, guidance, and support. Saying this affirmation will help you to activate angel power in your life by drawing God's holy angels near to you:

> "Angels, angels everywhere,
> protecting, guiding,
> and showing me they care!"

Chapter 2
Healing and Preparing Your Vibration

Discover how to clear, heal, energize, and protect your energy frequency to help you establish a strong and clear connection to the angels.

You have a unique energy frequency, otherwise known as your vibration and aura. Your aura is made up of several subtle bodies of energy, which incorporate your physical health, your emotional health, your mental health, and your spiritual health. To have a strong and vibrant energy frequency you therefore need to look after all equal parts of you so you can help to establish a good level of balance and harmony within your entire being. In this chapter we are going to discuss what can interfere with your energy frequency and weaken your overall aura power. When your aura power is weakened, your vibration will become slow and low, and this will interfere with the quality of your connection and clear communication with the angels.

You will be introduced to several easy but powerful exercises that can help you to clear, heal, energize, and protect your energy so that you can begin to maintain a healthy, balanced frequency. Doing these exercises will help you to regain power and strength within your aura, making it much easier for you to reach the angels' frequency. Not only that, if you begin to look after your overall energy vibration in this way, you will also help to ignite healing power on the physical level, improving any health conditions you currently have, easing any pain, and speeding up the healing of any injuries or illness.

Everything Is Energy

You are living in a world of unseen energies, an energetic matrix into which your *own energies* will pour into the universal mix in some way. It is very important to learn how to discern different kinds of energy so that you become aware of which energies can weaken you and which energies can help to support and strengthen you. You will then begin to consciously "take charge" of your aura, helping to naturally protect your energy so that it remains in a highly energized and vitalized state. A highly energized vibration is perfect for angel communication.

It is also important to add your own positive energy into the world, as this will help to diminish the mass consciousness of fear, one person at a time, and you will be participating with God's plan for peace on earth.

So what can interfere with our energy vibration and weaken us? The answer to this is psychic stress and energetic pollution. As we are energetic beings, our aura can become easily clogged and contaminated with an overload of psychic stress and energetic pollution. Psychic stress is created within our aura in a variety of ways, such as from the side effects of our own negative mind-set, our fears and worries, our mood swings, and our choice of an unhealthy lifestyle. Energetic pollution is absorbed into our aura from external sources such as other people's energies and the energies contained within the atmosphere and our environment. Our energy can also be compromised by low-level spirits and earthbound spirits, as their interference can drain us of our valuable energy and cause interference with our angelic connection. An accumulation of psychic stress and energetic pollution within our aura will begin to deplete our aura power and weaken us. This is why we need to regularly clear, heal, energize, and protect our vibration.

What Can Compromise the Energy of Our Physical Health?

Our Lifestyle

Our physical energy is compromised by our own free-will choice of an unhealthy lifestyle, by external sources of energetic pollution, and by interference of low-level spirits and earthbound spirits. When our physical energy is weak, we will feel fatigued, ill, and run down, and we can lack the physical energy we need to get us through the day. We also need to have plenty of energy for our body to naturally heal and repair itself, as our immune system will weaken when our energy is depleted. Lack of energy on the physical level will also interfere with our ability to create our dreams and desires, because it takes a good amount of aura power to do so.

Our lifestyle directly impacts our physical energy levels. We can breathe, absorb through our skin, and ingest energetic pollution into our body. Chemical toxins from the foods we eat and drink, the effects of smoking, the side effects of any medication, the toxins in the creams and lotions we use and in the cleaning products we use—all can interfere with the quality of our physical energy. The energetic side effects of overwork, lack of sleep, an unhealthy diet, lack of exercise and movement, dehydration, and any destructive habits and addictions will all help to create psychic stress and energetic pollution within our aura and diminish our physical energy levels.

Other People

At the physical level we will often encounter energetic pollution from other people. Energetic pollution can be considered to contain dirty, tired, toxic, and stagnant energies that can interfere with our aura power. Our aura is a highly sensitive and multidimensional energy field that interacts with all of life by transmitting and receiving energies continuously. Within the first layer of our aura we have seven main energy centers called *chakras*, and these chakras help to draw in energy from the universal supply to help sustain our physical health and well-being. Good, clean life-force energy will add to the vibrancy of our aura. Toxic, dirty, and stagnant life force will decrease the vibrancy of our aura.

All people, including ourselves, unconsciously transmit a certain amount of energetic pollution from their aura whenever they are overly negative, fearful, depressed, angry, emotionally drained, and/or physically sick. This contaminated life force will seep into the atmosphere around them, and if we are near and our aura power is low, we can easily absorb their psychic stress into our system. Our aura, when in good, healthy balance, will be able to deal with this, and will eventually process and clear the psychic stress from our system by transmuting what we need and by releasing what we don't. However, when we are continuously under stress, our aura becomes less able to do its job effectively, and then energetic contamination begins to build within our aura. We will lose aura power, and our physical energy levels will be low and easily drained. We can then experience symptoms such as fatigue, headaches, irritability, mood swings, and feeling overly sensitive.

Our Environment

Our home, our place of work, and anywhere we visit where there is a lot of human traffic can also contain energetic pollution within the atmosphere. This is due to the combined collective energies of everyone there, which accumulate and build in strength. Your home and work environment will vibrate at the frequency of all combined energies of those who live or work there; any arguments, fear, worry, and complaints will participate in creating varying degrees of energetic pollution. Even objects such as fluorescent lights, computers, wireless devices, and cell phones can all interfere with our energy field due to the electromagnetic radiation they emit.

Energetic pollution will naturally ground and become neutralized, or it will easily disperse or transform in time. Until that time, it can remain lingering in the atmosphere like an invisible toxic energy cloud. If our aura power is weak, then we will become energetically vulnerable and open to absorbing this energetic pollution into our aura, which can then zap our physical energy. Generally, the stronger the intensity of the accumulated energy held within the environment and atmosphere, the longer it will last. This is why you can feel eerie when you are in an area where there has been much pain and suffering, such as a battle ground or an old prison. There are also areas within our environment that will hold great spiritual power, which can be a wonderful tonic to our aura, helping us to feel energized whenever we visit there. You can even feel this way around certain people. Some people's energies will uplift you while others will drain you; it all depends on the overall energies that they carry within their aura. (Energetic pollution within your home can be cleared in numerous ways. This is often known as *space clearing*. See the end of this chapter for how to create the best atmosphere and vibration within your home to help you attract the angels.)

The following is a very powerful exercise to help you clear any accumulation of psychic stress and energetic pollution contained within your aura. This will help you quickly regain balance and harmony in your vibration, restore your aura power, and increase your physical energy levels.

Exercise:
Ground Your Energy and Make It Sparkle

✳ Visualize an energy bubble of vibrant white light or gold light surrounding your entire body and aura, and use the affirmation "Divine light protects me."

✳ Settle yourself into a comfortable breathing rhythm. Begin by taking a few long and slow deep breaths in through your nose and out of your mouth, as this will help get the energy flowing in your body. When you breathe in, imagine the aura around you expanding, and when you breathe out, feel yourself relaxing more deeply. Do this several times.

✳ Hold the mental intention that you are now going to clear your body and aura of all psychic stress and energetic pollution by grounding them.

✳ Focus your awareness on the soles of your feet and vividly imagine a tube of golden light coming from each foot and running deep down into the center of the Earth. These tubes of light are your *grounding cords*, and they are going to be used to empty any psychic stress and energetic pollution from your body and aura into the earth to ground and neutralize. (Please know that the earth itself will not be affected by these negative energies as the healing power of the Earth's energy will ground and neutralize them.) The gravity of the Earth is going to help to pull out the toxic low energies within your aura—just as a vacuum cleaner will suck up debris from the floor.

✳ Next, you are going to use the color gray to represent any psychic stress and energetic pollution. This will help you to easily visualize moving negative energies out of your system more effectively, as you cannot physically see energy.

✳ Let's begin. Mentally instruct that any psychic stress and energetic pollution held within your body and aura immediately leave you through your golden grounding cords. Visualize the psychic stress as a gray, smoky energy cloud as it moves from your body and aura and into the grounding cords; the grounding cords will quickly suck this energy away from you by sending it deep into the ground. This should take a few minutes.

✳ Once you have finished this process it is time to fill up your body and aura with new and vibrant energies. You will be using vitalizing energy from the Earth and also life-force energy from God. Red will be used as the color for Earth energy, which is very energizing, and white will be used as the color for life-force energy, which is vitalizing, purifying, and nourishing.

✳ Next, hold the mental intention that you are going to energize your body with Earth energy and life force energy.

✳ Visualize red Earth energy flowing up from the ground, up through your golden grounding cords, through the soles of your feet, up your legs, and then into the base chakra, which is your first main energy center located at the base of the spine. The base chakra will process this energy to help your body and aura. Now visualize some brilliant, white life-force energy flowing into your crown chakra, which is the energy center located at the top of your head. The crown chakra will process the white light and send it along the central energy channel in your body so that all the other chakras will receive some. You can also imagine your entire physical body and aura being bathed in purifying white light energy, helping to make your energy vibration sparkle.

✳ Finally, visualize your golden grounding cords releasing from your feet and disappearing into the ground, and then finish by repeating the following grounding affirmation three times: "I am clear, I am grounded, I am balanced." Well done—you have just actively helped to clear, heal, energize, and vitalize your body and aura!

———————

Psychic Attack

When other people talk negatively about you or are particularly angry with you, then they will assist in a process called *psychic attack*. It is called psychic attack because of the negative energy they give off concerning you. Their anger or general annoyance with you will help to create an energetic link directly into your own energy field, and you will become psychically attached and energetically bonded to each other. The negative energies they emit concerning you will then begin to filter through this psychic cord directly into your aura and will interfere with your own frequency. The stronger the intensity of the emotion directed to you, the more physical the effects of the psychic attack will be. Physical symptoms can vary, but most people will experience a headache, irritation, being overly emotional without knowing why, and feeling very fatigued. Your aura is usually your natural form of protection against phenomena such as psychic attack, but only when it is in a balanced and healthy state. When your aura power is weak, you diminish your protective shield and open yourself to the effects of any psychic attack.

If you feel or suspect that someone is sending you "bad vibes," you must never react by sending any negative energy back to the person, as this will continue to keep you energetically bonded to each other. To help you quickly cut the energetic cords between you, you need to rise above the issue by aligning with the power of Divine love. The energy of Divine love will empower your aura and will instantly dissolve the energetic cords of negativity existing between you. Use the power of Divine love to send the person positive energy by thinking of them in a loving, forgiving, and friendly way.

You can also send the person the blessing of Divine love, by asking God to bless her and to release her from your energy. You will usually find that when you do this the person will begin to change her behavior and attitude toward you, or will leave your life and no longer bother you. To help you connect with the energy of Divine love you can imagine yourself surrounded by a soft, pink bubble of light.

You can also imagine the other person surrounded by a bubble of soft, pink light so that the energy of Divine love can begin to soften her anger and annoyance with you. Knowing that other people's negativity can affect you in this way can help you be more mindful of how you think, feel, and talk about others.

Psychic attack can also happen when you spend your time around depressed, ill, or complaining people. These people need extra life-force energy to help sustain them, and they are happy to take yours whether they are consciously aware of doing so or not. They can siphon your life-force energy quite naturally, as their aura will act like a sponge ready to soak up and absorb any extra energy they can get. They will use this extra energy to temporarily sustain themselves until they are ready to use more appropriate ways to live and heal. A strong aura will help to deflect this form of attack, while a weakened aura will create the opening needed for that person to siphon your energy. The typical side effect of this kind of psychic attack is severe physical exhaustion. You may have heard of the term *psychic vampire,* which signifies a person who drains your energy in this way. To help you prevent your energy from being attacked in this way it is wise to regularly ground your energy so that you keep it balanced and strong. To protect your energy with Divine light, use the following powerful protection exercise.

Exercise:
Divine Light of Protection

The following exercise is short but very powerful, and it will help you to protect your energy. It offers you three easy ways to activate spiritual protection from a higher power. You can use the one you are most drawn too or use all three. Do this protection exercise daily, but always use it before you do any kind of energy work.

* Visualize an energy bubble of vibrant white light or gold light surrounding your entire body and aura and affirm that "Divine light protects me."

* Ask God for the white light of the Holy Spirit to surround and protect you from all forms of negative energy and affirm that "Divine light protects me."

* Ask your guardian angel to please watch over you and keep you safe from all harm, and affirm that "Divine light protects me."

Spiritual Attack

Earthbound spirits and low-level spirits can also interfere with your physical energy. Earthbound spirits are those spirits who haven't crossed over to the light for numerous reasons, including their own free will not to do so. They are not meant to exist on the Earth plane and so they need a steady supply of energy to help sustain them or they can quickly lose power. They can syphon our life-force energy if they happen to exist within the same space as we do and if our aura power is weak or imbalanced, as this will make it much easier for them to attach to us. They can also attach to our aura when we are emotionally vulnerable or ill, as our aura power is naturally diminished during those times.

Signs of earthbound spirits within the home often include missing items or misplaced items, electrical problems, heating problems, and plumbing problems. Another sign is a health condition that doesn't seem to improve because a person is being constantly drained of his or her energy; as previously mentioned, the body needs plenty of energy to be able to naturally heal itself. People may constantly find themselves having one cold after another or having a chest infection and cough that just doesn't seem to go away. Earthbound spirits can range from harmless, loving, and friendly spirits to not-so-nice or downright evil. This is because they are exactly the same in death as they were in life. However, even if they are nice and friendly, they can still drain your physical energy, as they are not meant to exist here.

Low-level spirits are those spirits who lack spiritual maturity and exist within the lower levels of the spiritual realm. Again, just as there are evil and not-so-nice people in the physical world, there are also evil and not-so-nice spirits in the spiritual realm. They are not able to enter the higher levels of the spiritual world until they have made amends and healed what they need to heal within their soul. Low-level spirits and earthbound spirits can be influenced by fallen angels to help play havoc on the Earth plane by trying to influence humans to do evil deeds. The good news is they have no power over the light, and they would not be able to influence someone who has developed his or her spiritual maturity and who acknowledges the light of God within him or her.

The only thing these low-level spirits can do is to try and interfere with your connection to the angels if you have not protected yourself with Divine light. All they can do is to try to pretend to be an angelic energy, but false guidance does not agree with Divine truth. You will discover more about false guidance and how to tell the difference in later chapters of this book. However, you are always in control, and you have more power over them than they have over you. You may never experience any interference from these spirits because your guardian angel does generally protect you, but sometimes they can get through because they exist on lower frequencies than do the angels.

You can easily send them on their way by commanding that they immediately leave you alone in the name and the power of Jesus Christ, which is the name above all names, and it will be done! The mighty and powerful Archangel Michael can also be invoked to remove any low-level spirits from your home and your aura. This mighty Archangel can help escort earthbound spirits and low-level spirits to the light. Archangel Michael can also use his sword of light to help cut any psychic cords of attachment to others or to cut the cords of attachment to any addictions and destructive habits you may have. You need to be serious in your intention to heal any addictions and habits for your request to activate spiritual power to help you. If you are of two minds you will simply delay spiritual help until you are truly ready to heal. Use the prayer requests at the end of this section to help you invoke the power of this magnificent Archangel.

You can attract earthbound or low-level spirits to you if you abuse substances such as drugs and alcohol as you open yourself up to the spiritual world. Drugs and alcohol will weaken your protection. You can also create problems if you meddle with things that you just do not understand and lack the spiritual maturity to deal with, such as using a Ouija board. It is not worth the risk of opening yourself up to negative spiritual forces that can interfere in your life.

Prayer Requests: Archangel Power

"Dear God, I ask for the assistance of the mighty and powerful Archangel Michael to intervene and remove all low-level spirits and earthbound spirits from interfering in my home, my aura, and my life by escorting them to their allocated dimension of light within the spiritual realm. Thank you, God, amen! And it is done!"

"Dear God, I ask for the assistance of the mighty and powerful Archangel Michael to cut the psychic cords of attachment to (say the person's name) for our greatest good. Thank you, God, amen! And it is done!"

"Dear God, I ask for the assistance of the mighty and powerful Archangel Michael to cut the psychic cords of

attachment to (name addiction or
destructive habit) for my greatest
good. Thank you God, amen! And it is
done!"

What Can Compromise the Energy of Our Emotional Health?

Emotional stress will energetically weigh heavily on
the aura, which will then interfere and even block
our connection to the angels because we will lack
aura power to reach them. Our emotional health is
compromised whenever we have any unresolved
emotions that we are either unaware of or are unable
to deal with. It is also compromised when our
energy is full of psychic stress and energetic pollution, and it is not grounded and cleared. When your
emotional energy is weak, you will feel overly sensitive, and easily overwhelmed, as if you were stuck
on an emotional roller coaster. Because your energy
is in desperate need of grounding, you may experience crying outbursts or angry outbursts, in your
body's attempt to release and clear the excess emotional energies. This is when the grounding exercise
is extremely useful for you to do.

You can even attack your own energy vibration,
by the negative way that you feel about yourself. If
you have any self-hatred and you are unable to love

and accept yourself, you will create emotional stress within your aura. You need to explore why you feel this way about yourself. The answer is often because of unresolved emotions. Unresolved emotions will often rise to the surface whenever you are experiencing similar emotional challenges in your present life circumstances, or when you confront a situation that invokes an old, painful emotion. This is an attempt for your conscious awareness to deal with the core issue so that you can heal it and clear it.

Emotional pain that you find too difficult to deal with, and which you are unwilling to let go of, can lead you to seek other ways to help you numb your pain or to keep it firmly buried. These ways are often very destructive for you because you need to expend a lot of energy to bury your emotions, or you need to find something potent enough to help numb them. The results of this can manifest as overwork, so that you are simply too busy to feel your pain, or unhealthy habits and addictions so that you can numb your pain.

Blocked emotions also lead to blocked creativity. If you do not allow yourself to feel your emotions, you will cause them to stagnate within your aura and this will weaken your aura power. You need plenty of aura power to be able to create your dreams and desires, and so you will often find that when you block your real feelings, you will also struggle in trying to create what it is you really want in your life. If you are currently struggling with creating your dreams or from achieving a greater level of inner peace, satisfaction, and fulfillment in your life, then you need to take a good honest look at your emotional health. Your emotional health is directly related to the state of your physical health and well-being. Depression, physical illness, and physical pain can be the result of blocked emotions, and so it makes sense to clear, heal, and balance your emotional energy regularly.

How to Heal Your Emotional Energy

Use the following powerful energy healing exercise to help you clear, heal, and balance your emotional health.

Exercise:
Angelic Ball of Divine Healing Light

* Protect your energy as previously shown.

* Settle yourself into a comfortable breathing rhythm. Begin by taking a few long and slow deep breaths in through your nose and out of your mouth, as this will help to get the energy flowing in your body. When you breathe in, imagine the aura around you expanding, and

when you breathe out, feel yourself relaxing more deeply. Do this several times.

✳ Ask your guardian angel to help you release any emotional stress and repressed emotions from your heart so that you can free your emotional energy to be able to heal. Your guardian angel is going to place a powerful ball of pink healing light energy into your heart chakra, which is located in the center of your chest. You are going to imagine yourself holding this pink ball of light in place with your hands.

✳ Next, rub your hands together and slightly cup them with your palms facing toward your body and holding them a few inches out from the center of your chest. Imagine that you are holding a pink ball of Divine healing light in place that is allowing your heart chakra to open, ready to release any emotional pain that you are willing to let go of. Your guardian angel will channel powerful healing energy through the minor chakras you have in the palms of your hands and into the ball of pink light. Stay like this for several minutes. You may feel a tingling response in your palms, you may feel as though you have pins and needles without the pain, or you may feel heat or coldness.

* Notice any old memories from your past resurfacing to your conscious mind as these will be clues to where any core emotional issues are first created. Simply be willing to allow healing energy to enter into these memories so you can clear and release them.

* You can also use this time to be specific about any emotional problems you are currently experiencing. Ask for help in releasing any heartache, grief, un-forgiveness, anger, or any other destructive emotions such as fear, jealousy, hatred, envy, low self-esteem, and self-hatred. At this point you may well release some tears, or you may physically shiver and shake. Emotional pain doesn't always get released in this way, but sometimes when emotions rise to the surface, they can cause a temporary reaction.

* To finish, simply bring your hands together into prayer position. Thank God and your guardian angel for the healing. Then shake your hands away from your body and down toward the ground. (This is known as an *energy break*.) Repeat the following affirmation three times: "Divine love heals me." Have a drink of water or a light snack to help ground your energy.

When You Find It Too Difficult to Forgive

Ask God to help you do what you find too difficult to do on your own. Use the power of prayer to ask for spiritual assistance and surrender all of your concerns to God. This will open a spiritual door for God and His angels to work within your life. This may include you getting some professional healing help to assist you in moving forward in your life, and you will be guided by a higher power to the right people who can help you. In Chapter 7, you will discover a powerful forgiveness exercise to do with the mighty and powerful Archangel Zadkiel.

What Can Compromise the Energy of Your Mental Health?

Our mental health is compromised when we are overly negative, when we have any limiting thoughts and beliefs, and when we are mentally stressed due to our fears, concerns, and pressures. When your mental energy is weak, you will feel mentally fatigued and clouded, have scattered thoughts, and will often be very forgetful. When you have too much on your mind, or you constantly live in your head by trying to analyze every single detail, your mental energy will be under pressure. Being under constant pressure can often cause us to have blood pressure problems and other health issues. When we are mentally imbalanced, our aura is severely drained of power, and we will interfere with our connection to the angels. Physical signs that you are mentally imbalanced can often manifest as constant headaches and anger, as these are your body's ways of trying to clear your negative mental energy. You can also be overly clumsy and accident prone because you are simply not grounded enough in your body.

Whenever you are mentally stressed you will be out of balance between the two cerebral hemispheres of your brain. The left hemisphere is typically concerned with your logical, rational mind, and the right hemisphere is typically concerned with your intuitive, creative mind. We need to have a healthy balance between both hemispheres to be able to be logical and creative at the same time; otherwise, we will diminish the full range of our mental power. We need our logical mind to get things done, and we need our creative mind to help inspire us with solutions and great ideas. Too much mental stress will cause us to lose this balance. Most people are more dominant in their left hemisphere due to their mental stress, and so they will unwittingly limit or block their creative power and intuition. We need to have a healthy balance of energy flowing between both hemispheres of our brain to create the optimum frequency for angelic communication to take place. Even if you are more creative than logical, you can still interfere with your angelic connection because you will still be out of balance between the two hemispheres. And you will limit your ability to reach the higher angelic frequencies because a balanced mind generates more power.

To help you achieve a good flow of energy between both hemispheres of your brain, it is a good idea to meditate. Meditation will help to calm your nervous system and you will feel lighter in your mental energy because of this. (You will be introduced to meditation in Chapter 4.) Physical exercise will also help you to naturally ground your mental stress, especially if it is done outdoors, such as walking or jogging. Fresh air, sunlight, and greenery are very cleansing for the mind and soul. You can also use the grounding exercise to help you ground the negative energies of your worries, fears, and concerns. Now you need to address any limiting thoughts and beliefs you have that interfere with your mental energy. The best way to do this is by using the power of affirmations.

*A*ffirmations

Affirmations are positive statements that can help uplift you and clear your mind of negative

energy. For healing purposes they wc
ing your negative, limiting thoughts ana
with the exact opposite, positive frequencies. If said
with a clear intent to heal, they can help you repro-
gram your mental energy so that your thoughts and
beliefs become in alignment with the affirmation.
A good technique to use is called *flip switching*, in
which you simply replace, or switch, your negative
thought patterns with healthy, new, positive ones.

Changing your thought patterns will help alter
your core beliefs. By doing this, you will begin to
notice a big difference in your mental health; you
will realize that you do not worry as much as you
once did, and you do not imagine or expect the
worst. Your whole outlook, perspective, and personality can change into a more positive, trusting,
and healthy state of being. And you will naturally
increase the strength and power in your aura. Use
the following easy technique to start clearing your
mental energy from today onward.

Flip-Switching Technique

Whenever you become aware of any negative
thinking, immediately replace your thoughts with
their exact opposite frequency and affirmation, even
though you don't yet believe them. (If you did, you
wouldn't be experiencing the thought in the first

place.) Retraining your brain definitely works over time and is something you should attempt to stick with. For example, if you have the thought "I am not good enough," immediately switch this thought to "I am good enough," and continue to do this until you feel differently about yourself and you notice that things have positively changed for you. This is when you will know that you have altered the core belief. If you have the thought "I am always unlucky," then immediately switch this thought to "I am very blessed." Do the same for all other limiting and negative thoughts. The whole point of this exercise is to help you become aware of your limiting thoughts and beliefs so that you take responsibility to clear and heal your mental energy, and regain balance and power in your aura.

Healing Unconscious Limiting Beliefs

It is possible for you to have unconscious limiting beliefs that can sabotage your dreams and desires and interfere with your angelic connection. For example, if you have the hidden belief that you are not spiritual enough, good enough, or intuitive enough to communicate with the angels, this can temporarily block your connection until you heal the belief. How do you heal these limiting beliefs if you don't know you have them? You will know when you have hidden limiting beliefs when you take a good, honest look at what is not working within your life, what you keep sabotaging in your life, and what you feel is preventing you from creating your dreams and desires. The biggest culprit is, quite often, fear. Use the following very powerful healing prayer to help you heal any unconscious limiting beliefs.

Healing Prayer

* While sitting in a relaxed and meditative state, feel yourself connected to and a part of Divine love. Divine love is compassionate, unconditional, forgiving, healing, energizing, peaceful, and comforting.

* State the following prayer request within your mind or out loud: "Dear God, I am willing to change my limiting thoughts and beliefs that I have, whether these be conscious or unconscious, and which interfere with my ability to achieve or receive. [Be specific.] I ask for the healing blessing of Divine love to please clear and heal my old limiting thoughts and beliefs so that I become in alignment with Divine truth." End with "Thank you, God, Amen!" or "It is done, it is done, it is done!"

What Can Compromise the Energy of Our Spiritual Health?

Many issues can compromise our spiritual health, the biggest being our false belief that we are separate from God and so we are unable to wake up to who we really are. The following issues will interfere with our spiritual development: lack of faith and belief in a higher power to help us; belief in our own power and our own self-importance for selfish gain; the false belief that we are separate from everyone else; refusal to take responsibility for our thoughts, words, and actions; and being out of alignment with Divine truth and Divine love. When our spiritual energy is weak we will lack faith, hope, and belief in a higher power to help us. In times of adversity we will lack the strength of spirit to help us get through the difficult times. We will have difficulty fulfilling our life purpose and will then focus on other unfulfilling ways to make a living. We will constantly be searching for our happiness instead of finding our happiness in our ability to be a channel for God's love and service to humanity. Our overall aura power will be weak, and this can typically affect our health, our well-being, the circumstances of our life, and our ability to connect to and communicate with the angels.

Expanding Our Consciousness

To expand our consciousness we need to understand more about who we really are. We are spiritual beings with a spiritual anatomy, and part of our spiritual anatomy includes our chakra system. Chakra healing is a very powerful process for developing our spiritual consciousness, which will then help us to raise our overall aura vibration. When our vibration is raised through spiritual growth and transformation, we will certainly help to increase our aura power. To be able to clearly hear, sense, and see the angels around us, we will need to clear and energize our chakras. This will enable us to reach higher frequencies and maintain our connection with the angels.

The Chakra System

The description of the chakras found here is simply an overview; entire books have been written about the chakras. The chakra system enables us to move energy throughout our aura and physical body. When we actively work with the chakras to clear and energize them, we can instantly increase our aura power. We have seven main chakras, which are located in the first subtle body of the aura, known as the *etheric body*. Each individual chakra spins and metabolizes energy at a certain frequency, and has its own individual color associated with it. We can use the individual color of each chakra to help us energize and balance the frequencies of that chakra. We can also use the color associated with each chakra as our central focus during a meditative state to open our chakras. This simply means it will help us expand our consciousness to connect with the angels. Closing our chakras therefore means we will bring our conscious awareness back into the physical dimension. Our chakras do not literally open and close, but they can become particularly blocked, disfigured, or stagnant; can spin too slowly or too quickly; and can spin in the wrong direction.

Each chakra looks like a mini tornado of swirling energies. Although they are located within the etheric subtle body, which is the first layer of our aura, they also extend outward to reach all seven subtle bodies of our aura. We have a central column of energy that runs up and down our spine, from the base of our spine to the crown of our head, and the roots of each chakra all connect into this central energy column. The crown chakra reaches upward toward the heavens and draws in life-force energy, Divine light, and spiritual guidance. The base chakra reaches downward toward the ground, helping to ground us to our lives and draws in Earth energy to help energize, vitalize, and ground us. The other five chakras are found in alignment running along the central energy column facing outward from the front of the body and into the aura. These five chakras also have their own counterparts on the back of the body, and they also face outward away from the body and into the aura.

Each chakra is concerned with an endocrine gland and nerve plexus, which is the direct connection the chakras have to the physical body. All chakras transmit and receive energies; indeed they can be likened to flash drives that hold and contain all information about us, even holding information about all of our past lives. When we consciously work with the energies of each chakra, we are able to expand our spiritual consciousness and grow through self-awareness, increasing in spiritual maturity and naturally building aura power. The following is a quick, basic introduction to the chakra system for the purpose of preparing you to clear, energize, and open them.

The 7 Main Chakras
The Base Chakra
* Located at the base of the spine.
* Energy color frequency is red.

✳ Related to our physical energy.

✳ Level of consciousness is connected to how well we manage our lives in the material world and our will to live. Do we feel safe and secure? Can we provide for our own basic needs? Do we accept other people's beliefs as our own without question? Do we have plenty of energy to participate fully in our lives and maintain our physical health?

✳ Vitalizes the body's adrenal glands.

The Sacral Plexus Chakra

✳ Located just below the navel.

✳ Energy color frequency is orange.

✳ Related to our emotional energy.

✳ Level of consciousness is connected to how well we manage our emotions and how well we use our creative energy. Do we allow ourselves to feel our emotions deeply, or do we repress our emotions? Are we carrying the emotional energy of guilt, sadness, grief, anger, hatred, and depression? What area of our life is no longer giving us emotional satisfaction and joy? Are we honoring our emotional health or

burying it? Do we allov
inspire our creative sp
need to do or be to he.ᵣ
ment?

* Vitalizes the body's gonads.

The Solar Plexus Chakra

* Located just above the navel.

* Energy color frequency is yellow.

* Related to our mental energy.

* Level of consciousness is connected to how
well we develop and manage our personal
power. Do we trust in our own power, or
do we allow others to overpower us? Are
we indecisive? Do we lack confidence in
our abilities and have low self-esteem? Do
we have any limiting beliefs?

* Vitalizes the body's pancreas.

The Heart Chakra

* Located in the center of the chest.

* Energy color frequencies are green and
pink.

* Related to our love for humanity and for
ourselves.

Level of consciousness is connected to how well we are able to give and receive unconditional love to others and ourselves. Do we have compassion for our fellow humans? Do we love and accept ourselves? Do we close our hearts to love for fear of being let down and hurt? Are we able to forgive?

* Vitalizes the body's thymus gland.

The Throat Chakra

* Located in the center of the throat.

* Energy color frequency is blue (more toward turquoise blue).

* Related to the clear expression of our will for our life and the Divine will for our life.

* Level of consciousness is connected to how well we manage our self-expression by learning how to live our truth and communicate our truth to others. When we grow in spiritual maturity we will align more with Divine will than with our own will. Do we find it easy to personally express our truth to others? Do we acknowledge the truth of our heart and soul? Are we living a lie in any area of our life?

* Vitalizes the body's thyroid gland.

The Third Eye Chakra

* Located in the center of the forehead.

* Energy color frequency is indigo.

* Related to our intuition, spiritual insight, and clarity of mind (our higher mind and mental energy).

* Level of consciousness is connected to the development of our spiritual insight and the ability to use this spiritual wisdom within our life. Are we able to see material life problems and concerns with a greater spiritual perspective? Are we able to understand mental concepts clearly and easily? Are we able to see clearly (visualize) what course of action we need to take?

* Vitalizes the body's pituitary gland.

The Crown Chakra

* Located at the top of the head.

* Energy color frequencies are violet and white.

* Related to the integration of our spiritualty and our understanding that we are all part of the one Divine consciousness.

* Level of consciousness is connected to how well we develop and manage our

spiritual maturity by integrating all parts of us: physical, emotional, mental, and spiritual. Are we open to deepening our relationship with a higher power to attain spiritual wisdom? Do we have faith and trust in God and Divine guidance?

* Vitalizes the body's pineal gland.

Exercise: Clearing Your Chakras

The following exercise will help you to clear, heal, and energize your chakras, which will help you expand your overall consciousness and give power to your aura.

* Protect your energy as previously described.

* Settle yourself into a comfortable breathing rhythm. Begin by taking a few long and slow deep breaths in through your nose and out of your mouth; this will help to get the energy flowing in your body. When you breathe in, imagine the aura around you expanding, and when you breathe out, feel yourself relaxing more deeply. Do this several times.

* Place your awareness on your crown chakra (top of the head), and ask for the white light of the Holy Spirit to enter into this chakra and

clear it of anything that is not in alignment with Divine wisdom. Affirm that "my beliefs are in alignment with Divine wisdom."

✳ Next, place your awareness on your third eye chakra (center of the forehead), and ask for the white light of the Holy Spirit to enter into this chakra and clear it of anything that is not in alignment with Divine insight. Affirm that "my intuition is in alignment with Divine insight."

✳ Next, place your awareness on your throat chakra (center of the throat), and ask for the white light of the Holy Spirit to enter into this chakra and clear it of anything that is not in alignment with Divine truth. Affirm that "I am in alignment with Divine truth."

✳ Next, place your awareness on your heart chakra (center of the chest), and ask for the white light of the Holy Spirit to enter into this chakra and clear it of anything that is not in alignment with Divine love. Affirm that "I am in alignment with Divine love."

✳ Next, place your awareness on your solar plexus chakra (just above the navel), and ask for the white light of the Holy Spirit to enter into this chakra and clear it of anything that is not in alignment with Divine knowledge. Affirm that "I am in alignment with Divine knowledge."

✳ Next, place your awareness on your sacral plexus chakra (just below the navel), and ask for the white light of the Holy Spirit to enter into this chakra and clear it of anything that is not in alignment with Divine feelings. Affirm that "I am in alignment with Divine feelings."

✳ Next, place your awareness on your base chakra (base of the spine), and ask for the white light of the Holy Spirit to enter into this chakra and clear it of anything that is not in alignment with Divine strength. Affirm that "I am in alignment with Divine strength."

✳ Finally, visualize your entire body and aura fill up with soft pink light. You have now made an important energetic shift toward achieving a faster and lighter frequency.

Opening Your Chakras

The following exercise is quick and easy, and it will help you to quickly expand your consciousness and give instant power to your aura ready for angel communication. You will be asked to open and close your chakras during later chapters of this book when it is time for you to spiritually hear, sense, and see the angels around you. The purpose of this exercise is to help you to become comfortable in opening and closing the chakras. Remember: opening the chakras will enable you to expand your consciousness to receive higher spiritual guidance, and closing your chakras will enable you to close down your consciousness so that you become grounded and centered.

* Protect your energy as previously described.

* Settle yourself into a comfortable breathing rhythm. Begin by taking a few long and slow deep breaths in through your nose and out of your mouth, as this will help to get the energy flowing in your body. When you breathe in, imagine the aura around you expanding, and when you breathe out, feel yourself relaxing more deeply. Do this several times.

* You are going to open your chakras from the base to the crown by visualizing each one as spinning around in a clockwise direction (as if you were the face of the clock) and expanding. Use the color of each chakra to help you keep your focus strong: red, orange, yellow, green, turquoise blue, indigo, violet. This will only take a few minutes. Use the following easy guidelines to do so.

* Place your awareness on your base chakra located at the base of the spine and visualize the chakra as a bright red light. Imagine it beginning to spin in a clockwise direction, increasing in speed and size so that it begins to expand outward into your aura. Affirm that "my base chakra is now open."

* Using orange light in the area of your sacral plexus chakra (just below the navel), do the same thing and affirm that "my sacral plexus chakra is now open."

* Using yellow light in the area of your solar plexus chakra (just above the navel), affirm that "my solar plexus chakra is now open."

* Using green light in the area of your heart chakra (center of the chest), affirm that "my heart chakra is now open."

* Using turquoise blue light in the area of your throat chakra (center of your throat), affirm that "my throat chakra is now open."

* Using indigo light in the area of your third eye chakra (center of your forehead), affirm that "my third eye chakra is now open."

* Using violet light in the area of your crown chakra (top of your head), affirm that "my crown chakra is now open."

Once your chakras are open you have prepared your vibration to receive angelic guidance. The following chapters will help you to understand the way in which guidance is delivered and received. There are two easy ways that you can use to close down your chakras, and it is a good idea to try both.

2 Easy Ways to Close Your Chakras

* Beginning at the crown chakra and ending at the base chakra, simply place your focus on each chakra individually by using its associated color and visualize it returning to a slower speed and smaller size. When you have finished, use the affirmation "I am grounded." Have a drink of water or a light snack to help ground your energy.

* Visualize intense white light pouring into your crown chakra and traveling through the central energy column, which each individual chakra connects into, until it reaches your base chakra. The white light will help return your chakra frequencies back to their normal rates and sizes so that

you will remain in a healthy, balanced state. When you have finished, use the affirmation "I am grounded." Have a drink of water or a light snack to help ground your energy.

Everything you have discovered within this chapter will help you prepare and maintain a good quality vibration. Now all you need to do is set the scene to help you create an angel-friendly atmosphere within your home.

Creating an Angel-Friendly Atmosphere

To work with the angels it is best to create an energized and elevated energy frequency within your home, as this will help to bring the angels near. The following list will give you some ideas about what you can do to help you create an angel friendly atmosphere:

* Create a space that is clutter free, dust free, and quiet, and one that has natural lighting. De-clutter your entire household; a clean and tidy house will help to raise the vibration of the whole home.

* Clear away any computers, phones, and other forms of electromagnetic stress within your chosen space, as this stress can interfere with your connection to the angels.

* Add healing crystals. Rose quartz and selenite are good choices. Rose quartz will help you open your heart chakra, and selenite will help you open the crown chakra so that your consciousness can move into the higher realms and angelic world.

* Add fresh-cut flowers, as the life force will be strong and they will emit a positive frequency. Include other high-vibrational and power objects within your space, such as pictures of Jesus, spiritual books, spiritual quotes, and any other symbols of unconditional love.

* Use incense to help clear the space you are going to use. (White sage is good.) You can also waft this incense all over your aura from your head to your feet, over your chakras, and around the outline of your body. This will help clean and prepare your energy vibration for angel communication.

* Play soft, healing music in the background to help elevate the vibration in the room.

* Light a white candle as a blessing and say a prayer of protection before you begin any form of angelic communication or meditation.

Angel communication will be much easier for you whenever your own vibration and the vibration of your home are both clear and vibrant. To finish this chapter I will leave you with a powerful prayer of protection:

> "Dear God, I ask for the powerful white light of the Holy Spirit to surround and protect me and for my guardian angel to keep me safe from all harm. Let Divine light shine throughout my home, clearing away all low vibrations and energizing it with the power of Divine love. Thank you, God, Amen."

Chapter 3
Angel Signs and Messages

Make yourself familiar with the angels
and behold them frequently in spirit;
for without being seen, they are present
with you.

— St. Francis De Sales

The angels are very happy to leave us signs of
their presence, as they know that we often need to
have tangible evidence to help reinforce our belief in
them. Different kinds of signs left by the angels can
offer us helpful messages, insights, and guidance,
which will always be for our greatest good. Signs will
eventually become less frequent and less important
to you when you no longer need to receive them in
order to know that you are being helped—unless of
course they are used by the angels to reveal a specific

message to you. However, signs are nothing in and of themselves; they are simply helpful reminders that God is watching over us. Signs left by the angels are meant to help stir and awaken our intuitive nature so that we can expand our conscious connection and deepen our relationship with a higher power.

The power is not within the sign itself; the power is within the message that the sign reveals. The intention of the angels through using specific signs to reach you is to help to comfort you, encourage you, inspire you, support you, prepare you, uplift you, strengthen your faith when needed, and reveal specific guidance and information to you—all on behalf of God. The angels will never leave you any signs that will cause you any fear or alarm; if you do feel this way, you can be sure that it is your ego and your imagination at play.

How will you know that a sign is especially for you? You will know by the message the sign reveals to you, and how the message makes you feel within your heart and soul. Signs, often are delivered when you have already asked God or the angels for their help. Notice how you feel when you receive it; you can feel supported, uplifted, and renewed with faith that all will be well. Within this chapter you are going to discover the array of signs and messages that the angels can bring us to help alert us to their presence, to help give us insight and guidance, and to help nudge us along our life path. Angelic guidance can help you within all areas of your life, but remember that you need to ask for this help.

*A*ngel Nudges

Nudges from the angels are mostly delivered through your intuitive nature. The angels can nudge you to read a specific book, watch a certain film, or pay attention to a stranger's conversation; or you can be nudged to meet a certain person. Angels do this because they know that there is something good for you to find there, some important piece of information, relevance, or significance that is just for you. Pay attention to any intuitive flashes of wisdom you receive, as this will be your guardian angel attempting to nudge you in the right direction. An intuitive flash of wisdom can be likened to a *light bulb moment*, when an inspirational idea or the answer to what you have been searching for immediately springs into your conscious mind.

*B*utterflies

Butterflies are a sign that the angels are all around you. One butterfly can represent your guardian angel, and a number of butterflies can signify that several angels are close by. Angels will bring you the sign of a butterfly, or a number of butterflies, when you are grieving the loss of a loved one to let you know that your loved one is safe and well, and is close by. Watch to see if the butterfly lands on your shoulder or flies right in front of your face. If so, you are being lovingly touched or kissed by an angel.

Butterflies can also symbolize a need for freedom from whatever is keeping you prisoner in your life and a time for you to experience new beginnings. This often includes a need for freedom from any destructive habits or behaviors, limiting beliefs, and emotional issues that no longer serve you. The angelic message of the butterfly symbolizes a need for you to keep your faith strong during times of difficult transitions. The angels want you to know that painful moments and struggles are only temporary and life will soon improve. In many cultures the butterfly is associated with the soul. Our spiritual evolution requires our soul to shine and emerge in beauty through spiritual growth and transformation, just as a butterfly emerges from its chrysalis to fly free from it temporary restriction.

*D*ragonflies

A dragonfly is also a sign that your guardian angel is around you, especially when there is reference to its wings. The angelic message of the dragonfly symbolizes that you will experience significant life changes through the process of self-realization, self-awareness, and spiritual maturity. You are searching for a deeper meaning and purpose in your life, and you are on a journey of self-discovery. If someone has experienced loss or sadness of some kind, then the angelic message of the dragonfly is to accept change and to move forward gracefully.

Robins
Angels will bring you the sign of a robin redbreast to signify a period of joyful new beginnings. You will soon be celebrating, happy, and uplifted. Angels can also send you the sign of the robin when you are going through the healing process of losing a loved one to help comfort you. The angelic message of the robin is to let you know that your spirit loved one is safe and well, and is still around you. If you have dreamed of your spirit loved one and then you see the sign of a robin, this will be your confirmation that your dream was a real spiritual visit from him or her. The love you once shared together on Earth will continue on for eternity.

White Doves
White doves are sent by the angels to bring you the sign of inner peace. If something has been

troubling you and you have lost your inner peace, then the angelic message of the white dove is to let you know that there are peaceful solutions to your problems. Doves carry the symbolism of gentle care, peace, love, and purity. If you see any doves, especially white doves, then the angels want you to nurture yourself and take care of your well-being. If you have been overly stressed, under pressure, or worn out, then you need to take a break, slow down, and have some time off to help you renew your spirit and revitalize your energy. In doing so, you will regain a peaceful level of harmony and tranquility in your soul.

*A*ngel Objects

Angel ornaments, statues, art, and jewelry can be found literally everywhere. It's no coincidence that these angelic delights appear to you in your daily life. Finding angel objects or receiving angel objects can be a gentle nudge from your guardian angel to let you know that it wants to connect with you. Angel objects are signs that your guardian angel is around you. Any kind of angelic object, statue, ornament, or jewelry will hold a positive, high vibration of light energy. This is because of the powerful collective belief (consciousness) in the goodness of angel beings as a divine force. The angelic message in receiving any type of angel object is that you are being divinely protected by your guardian angel and other angelic beings.

Coins

Angels love to leave us coins, also known as *pennies from heaven*, as a sign that they are aware of our material life concerns. They want to help uplift you and for you to know that a higher power is watching over you. Your finances will soon improve or you will be helped in some material way, which will help your circumstances to improve.

Films of Angels

Films of angels are also signs that the angels are close by and giving you a friendly hello. A classic angel film titled *It's a Wonderful Life* tells a great story about a trainee angel named Clarence. Clarence is not the typical kind of angel you would imagine, in that he doesn't appear with wings, but as a normal-looking human being. Heaven sends him to help a young man who wishes that he had never been born. If Clarence can reach the young man and help him to *see the light*, then he will get to earn his "angel wings." This remarkable film has many symbolic and subtle messages from the angels. Whoever wrote the film must have been influenced by the angelic kingdom to create such an inspirational, uplifting, and heart-warming story. My favorite line from the entire film is "Every time a bell rings an angel gets his wings." I always smile and think of Clarence the trainee angel whenever I hear a bell ringing. If you are watching a film about angels or one that has angelic references in it, pay attention to the moral and essence of the story, as it may reveal some significant information, insight, and guidance for you.

Angel Music

Angels can bring you intuitive messages through the avenue of music and in the lyrics of a song. References to angels in the lyrics of a song are also a sign that your guardian angel is close by. Music is very powerful. The angels know what songs hold certain memories for you, and they will often use these songs to help reach you. If you just happen to switch on the radio and you hear a song playing that connects you to your spirit loved one, this is typically a personal sign from him to tell you he is still with you, he loves you, and he can feel your love for him. Music is good for the soul, and the angels congregate wherever beautiful music is playing. The musical instrument the harp is a symbolic sign of angelic energy working within your life.

*A*ngel Dreams

Angels will use our dream state to help reveal some significant insight into what we need to do within our daily life to help us sort out any problems. They will also help our spirit loved ones to enter into our dreams so that we can reconnect with them during our sleep. Have you ever had a dream in which you have been flying through the sky? If so, this is a sign that you are on an astral visit to meet with your guardian angel, guide, or spirit loved ones. Sometimes our dreams are the only way for our guardian angel to get through to us, especially if we are particularly stressed, overly busy, or off balance in any way, as this will interfere with our ability to notice any signs, messages, and nudges in our daily life that are sent to help us.

A sure sign that you have received an angelic dream is when the dream is vivid in nature, and when the emotional intensity of your dream stays with you for quite some time, whereas other dreams will easily fade away from your memory. Angels can appear in your dream if they desire, but it is usually the *essence of your dream* that the angels will use to deliver their angelic message to you. You can ask your guardian angel to visit you in your dreams or to help reveal some significant information you need to know. Keep a pen and pad by the side of your bed so you can record any insight you receive in your dreams upon awakening.

Feathers

Feathers appear when angels are near.

Feathers are extremely significant when it comes to the angels, with white feathers being the most recognized and universal angel sign. However, the angels will certainly use all kinds of colored feathers to let you know they are around you and to help reveal specific messages to you. Feathers can appear anywhere and everywhere, as the angels can easily leave them along your path. They can be found in the home, in your place of work, in the street, or any place you happen to visit. Feathers landing on you or blowing toward you so that you can literally catch them is a sure sign that the angels have heard your requests loud and clear.

Many small white feathers found together suggest a number of angels are surrounding you, including your guardian angel. Large feathers can be left by the mighty and powerful Archangels. I have personally found feathers in my bedroom, in my car, on the airplane, and even at the movies. Angels will use any types of feathers to bring you a sign, or they can even manifest feathers when there aren't any nearby for them to access. Angels will use feathers from our own pillows and duvets, from birds of any size, or even from artificial ones, such as those from a feathered boa.

Where you find feathers can also be very significant. Feathers left in the car will be a sign to offer you protection on your journey. Feathers left by the side of the bed can be a sign that an angel has visited you in your dreams or has given you healing energies during your sleep. Feathers found in the hospital can be a sign that the angels are helping to heal a sick loved one. Angels just love to leave us feathers, as each feather can also have a special intuitive meaning based on its specific color vibration.

Following is a list of different colored feathers and their intuitive messages. You can use this as a reference whenever you find a specific colored feather or as an intuitive exercise right now to help you gain a deeper insight into what is currently happening in your life. Simply ask your guardian angel to help you with a specific issue you need some guidance with, and then read through each colored feather meaning. If any intuitive messages stand out (words coming to life just for you), pay close attention to the guidance they offer. This is a fun, insightful, and powerful way to receive intuitive messages from the angels.

White Feathers

White feathers are left in your path as a sign or calling card from the angels. All angels will use white feathers as an initial sign, because most of us associate angels with white-feathered wings. This is based on our perception of angels, so they will use what they know is most comfortable for and acceptable to us. When you receive a white feather you can be certain that the angels are working behind the scenes of your life to help you. Your connection with them has begun, and they have heard your request. Angels want you to be uplifted by the sight of these white feathers and to have the faith and belief that they are near. If you ask your guardian angel to give you a sign that it is with you, then most likely your guardian angel will leave you a white feather to help you strengthen your belief in it.

The intuitive message of a white feather signifies your need to elevate your energy frequency to a whole new level. This will help you improve any health conditions you currently have, and attract and create positive new experiences into your life. Your guardian angel is aware of your desire to spiritually progress and is happy to help you. This will require you to do some energetic "detoxing" so that you can rid your aura of as much psychic stress (which only serves to hold you back), as you can. It is time to

make your life more simplistic so that you ⟨
some much-needed inner peace and joy. Start by
evaluating your entire life, and then begin to weed
out what no longer serves your greatest good. Do
you surround yourself with too many negative and
draining people? Do you spend your time staying in
a relationship or job that no longer fulfills you? Do
you ignore your dreams and desires for fear of failure? If so, it is time to make significant life changes
to help you clear the energetic blocks from your life's
path. Brush away the old stagnant energies from
your life to help make room for new beginnings to
unfold.

To help you elevate your aura frequency you also
need to take responsibility for your physical health.
Eating a healthy, balanced diet; hydrating your body
with good, clean water; making time in your day for
regular exercise; and having enough rest and sleep
will all help you to detox your body and aura. Exercis-
ing is particularly good for you because moving your
body will help you shake off stagnant energies, which
will then naturally ground you. Establishing healthy
daily life routines will keep your energies humming
and vitalized. Getting enough restful sleep will help
to restore your body's energy levels. Finding a white
feather signifies that it is time to meditate regularly, as
this will help you to clear the energy of your mind/
body/spirit and elevate your aura frequency.

Red Feathers

The intuitive message of a red feather directly relates to your physical energy levels, your current life circumstances, and your health. You are currently losing much-needed energy due to your fearful concerns and lack of motivation and ambition in your life. This lack of energy can affect both your health and your life circumstances. You need to have plenty of energy for your body to heal and repair itself. You also need to have plenty of energy to build enough aura power to be able to create positive new experiences, but you are simply too tired to do so. Are you overly concerned with your finances? Do you have problems at work or in getting work, and therefore lack hope for your own future? Do you have issues with your property, moving, or renovations of some kind? Do you have physical pain or health conditions that don't seem to improve with medical help? If so, the angels want to help you free your stuck energy so that you can regain your power and strength to improve your health, well-being, and life circumstances.

It is time to change your perspective to a more positive outlook so that you begin to expect that things will work out for you. This will help to activate angel power within your life. Material life struggles are only temporary, and they can and will improve over time. In the meantime you may need to accept certain conditions as they are, but with an attitude of gratitude for what you already have in your life that brings you joy and that meets your basic needs. Evaluate any limiting beliefs you have that may be holding you back. Keep on believing and moving forward toward the creation of your dreams and desires by taking any small steps that will enable you to develop your unique gifts and talents.

To help you free your stuck energy, you need to do what you can to move your body more. Physical exercise can help increase the flow of energy around your body and aura. Also, do the grounding exercise from Chapter 2 to help rid your aura of any excess fear and stress. Be more ambitious in your outlook and believe that the angels can guide you with any material life concerns if you ask them for help. Finding a red feather intuitively signifies that it's now time for you to have courage, strength, and endurance to win through.

Orange Feathers

The intuitive message of an orange feather is connected to your emotional health. It is time for you to face, feel, and then free your emotional pain, and regain a new level of joy and creativity in your life. Emotional stagnation is affecting your life. This can be connected to the energetic side effects of low self-esteem, mood swings, and depression. Are you currently going through a divorce or separation? Are you grieving the loss of a loved one? Are you experiencing a material loss of some kind, such as a financial or business loss? Are you constantly reliving the pain of your past and experiencing unresolved emotions such as guilt, anger, and un-forgiveness?

Your emotional stagnation is beginning to block the flow of joy from entering your life. You are temporarily also blocking your own creative energy from flowing and being able to create new expressions of joy and fulfillment. When you lose your creative spark you will feel a deep level of sadness within your soul because your natural state of being is to create your life anew through using your unique gifts and talents.

We all need time to process our feelings and heal, but if we refuse to move forward in our lives, our depressed state of being can eventually become normal to us. It will then become much harder for us to climb out of our despair. The angels are aware that you are now ready to move forward again in your life to experience a new level of joy in your heart and soul, and they want to help you to do so. It is now time for you to ask your guardian angel for help with what you are having emotional difficulty with. (Also

use the emotional healing exercise from Cha┌
God never gives you more than you can handle,
and God is giving you the strength and the courage
you need through His angels, to rise above your
difficulties and to regain balance of your emotions.
Finding an orange feather intuitively signifies that
it's now time for you to take small creative steps
toward reaching your deepest dreams and desires.

Yellow Feathers

The intuitive message of a yellow feather is
directly related to your mental energy and your personal power. It is now time to become a more con-
fident and powerful you by changing any limiting
beliefs that do not serve your greatest good and by
changing any negative thought patterns you currently have into more positive ones. Fear and worries will certainly weaken your personal power.
Have your prior life experiences determined your
self-worth? Do you lack belief and confidence in
your own gifts and talents? Are you indecisive, and
do you find it hard to trust in your own decisions?
Do you allow others to easily overpower and manip-
ulate you? If so, you have the power to change all of
this by directly working with your mental energy.
(See Chapter 2.)

The angels want you to know that it is now time for you to develop and expand your self-awareness, which will increase your personal power, and help you to believe in yourself. When you develop your personal power you will also increase the power within your aura to be able to create your dreams and to align with your life purpose. You will become less indecisive and less reliant on others to give you advice, as you will learn to listen to and depend on your own personal knowledge and wisdom. Developing your personal power will also help strengthen your natural intuitive nature and gut instinct. You will soon have an opportunity to empower yourself through study, especially in connection with what you desire to eventually do and become. Allow this new knowledge to integrate into your life to help you become a strong, more self-aware, and balanced individual. Finding a yellow feather intuitively signifies that it's now time for you to increase your knowledge and heal limiting beliefs to help you in your path of spiritual growth and transformation.

Green Feathers

The intuitive message of green feather is directly related to the unconditional love you have for others and for humanity. You are a peace-maker and a natural healer; you have great compassion in your heart and soul for others and for the world itself. Because you are so compassionate and empathic, you can often absorb the emotional pain of others and from the low vibrational energies in the environment. To help you balance the energies of your aura, you need to take regular walks outside to clear away any energetic stress and to help revitalize you. Because you are very sensitive you can become easily drained and fatigued when you allow other people's energies to overwhelm you and drain you.

Do you have a problem keeping energetic boundaries and find it difficult to say no to people? Do you have a problem establishing a healthy, balanced daily life routine? Do you have a problem receiving from others because you are always inclined to "give, give, give"? The angels want you to know that it is okay for you to also receive, and that when you allow yourself to receive from others, it will help to increase the abundance in your life because your aura power will become balanced in the dual energies of giving and receiving. It is also time for you to set healthy boundaries so that your health and well-being remain strong. When you do this you will have more energy to help others in a more appropriate and healing way. Finding a green feather intuitively signifies that it's now time for you to establish a healthy balance within your life.

Pink Feathers

The intuitive message of a pink feather is related to the amount of unconditional love you have for yourself. It is time for you to step up your inner healing by learning how to fully love and accept yourself exactly as you are. You are compassionate toward others but less so to yourself. The angels want to bring your attention to the way that you think and feel about yourself. It is time for you to become more unconditionally loving toward yourself. The angels know that this will help you to spiritually grow and transform your aura vibration. Treat yourself the same way that you would treat someone you love. Replace any self-criticism with loving, kind thoughts and this will help elevate your moods.

Are you happy to give emotional support to others, but do you find it difficult to let other people in to help emotionally support you? Are you lonely and desirous of a romantic and loving relationship, but you never seem to meet anyone? Do you find it difficult to form trusting and long-lasting friendships because you fear you will get hurt? Have you been heartbroken in a previous relationship and so you fear getting hurt again? If so, you have built an invisible energetic wall of protection around you that will help to repel real love from entering your life. If you hold any anger, resentment, and fear in your heart due to previous relationships, you will attract other relationships that match your expectations so that your beliefs are reinforced. To attract love, you will need to heal the issues of your heart so that you can open it once more.

When you learn to love and accept yourself you will begin to open your heart to help you attract love into your life. Allow others to form close and loving relationships with you without the fear of getting hurt or heartbroken. Ask the angels to help you heal the emotional pain carried deep within your heart so that you can fully give and receive love again. Finding a pink feather signifies that it is now time for you to love and accept yourself for who you are, and to open your heart to receive love.

Blue Feathers

The intuitive message of blue feather is directly related to your creative expression. There is a need for you to align your will with the will of God so that you can discover a greater level of joy and happiness in your life. When you surrender your life to God, you will be used as a channel to represent and communicate God's love in the world through your own form of creative self-expression. It is time to make greater use of your creative gifts and talents, which can be of service to others and to the world. The angels want to bring your awareness to acknowledge and live the truth of your heart over the fears of your head so that you can expand your spiritual potential. When you learn to live your truth you begin to spiritually mature, and you will do unto others as you would have others do unto you.

Do you ignore the truth in your heart because you fear failure or you fear what others might say? Are you living a lie in any area of your life? If so, you need to examine what you have been ignoring so that you can begin to make significant life changes that will eventually bring you a deeper level of happiness. Are you living your life to your greatest potential, or are you living your life in a small and unassuming way? You are meant to create, you are meant to shine, and you are meant to remember who you really are. You are a Divine spark of God, and you have God's creative power within you. When you align your will with the will of God, you will co-create greater levels of joy in the world and in your life. God has a great plan for your life, but you first need to be ready and willing to do what it takes for you to go to the next level so that you can expand your spiritual consciousness. Living your truth at this level requires you to take responsibility for living your life in accordance with your level of spiritual maturity. Your life needs to be a reflection of your spiritual progression.

If it isn't, what you believe is true within you will not be truthfully expressed within your daily life. Finding a blue feather signifies that it is now time to live your truth.

Indigo and Purple Feathers

The intuitive message of the indigo and purple feather is related to the insight you currently have and are continuing to develop about your life, the world, and a higher power. However, the angels want to bring your attention to your present mental concepts that are interfering with your ability to gain a greater clarity of mind. Do you worry about your future? Do you imagine negative and fearful things happening to you or your loved ones? Do you lack spiritual insight about reality, your life purpose, and your place in the world? Are you able to rise above your dramas, adversities, and other stressful issues to perceive these problems with a greater perspective? It is time for you to look at things differently and to acknowledge your own interference in forming these mental concepts so that you can begin to visualize and think in a more enlightened manner.

This newfound clarity of mind will also help you to gain deeper insight into and perspective of your relationship with a higher power, and you will continue to expand your consciousness. You are at the stage of your life when you are strengthening your intuitive nature to be able to receive clear insight from a higher power to help yourself and others. Your spiritual path is expanding, and new and exciting areas of metaphysical study entice you. Finding an indigo or purple feather at this time suggests that you need to expand your vision for yourself and for your role within the world. Dream big, and use your enlightened insight to serve others who are on the same path as you but who are less enlightened. Meditation and visualization work will help you expand your spiritual focus.

Violet and Lilac Feathers

The intuitive message of the violet and lilac feather is related to your connection and relationship with a higher power. The angels are helping to guide you in your spiritual development. You are ready to go to the next level by increasing your spiritual knowledge and wisdom, and then applying it to your life. To do this you need to work on the integration of your whole being so that you build plenty of aura power to be able to elevate your vibrational frequency. Your physical, emotional, mental, and spiritual health need to be balanced and integrated. It is now time to work on improving any issues in any of these areas that do not agree with Divine truth and Divine love. In doing so, you will begin to increase the amount of light held within your aura. The amount of light you hold within your aura will reward you with greater responsibility as a representative of God's power and love, and this is what will take you to the next level.

Use your aura power wisely to help lead and guide others toward developing their own spirituality and connection to a higher power. Living your life by shining your light brightly into the world will set a good example to others who have lost their way or are spiritually sleeping. We are all connected; it is our life purpose to serve and help others to remember who they really are so they can also shine brightly with the power of God's love. The light that you shine will allow others to see that it is also possible for them to change their own destructive behaviors, patterns, and limitations. Finding a violet or lilac feather signifies that new spiritual knowledge and wisdom are coming your way to help you spiritually grow and transform your soul. Make prayer and meditation part of your daily practice to help keep your aura power strong.

Brown Feathers

The intuitive message of a brown feather is related to your grounding within the world. The angels want to bring your awareness to your need to remain grounded and present in your daily life. You are currently on an emotional merry-go-round, and your mood swings, worries, and fears are preventing you from living fully in the moment. In what area of your life do you feel out of balance? It is important to bring your awareness back into the present moment so that you have enough energy and aura power to make positive life changes and improve any physical health complaints you currently have. You often worry about the future, or you live in the past by going over your emotional pain or the mistakes you once made. You are very rarely focused in the present, so you can become clumsy, disorganized, constantly late, and unfocused. It is time for you to ground your energy.

To help you ground your energy you can connect with nature and do some form of physical exercise. The healing energy you receive from nature can help to clear your aura of psychic stress and bring you clarity of mind and a new perspective. When you bring your awareness back into the present moment, you will create a clear space for your guardian angel to deliver a spiritual solution to any problems or worries that have been consuming you. Physical exercise will help you to shake off stagnant energies and get energy flowing around your body without restrictions. Think of grounding in terms of your physical existence and do what you can to gain a healthy balance in your daily life routine. Eat a healthy, balanced diet and drink plenty of clean water to hydrate your body. Use the grounding exercise in Chapter 2 to help you. Finding a brown feather signifies your need to remain grounded in the present moment.

Gray Feathers

The intuitive message of a gray feather is related to your physical health and well-being. The angels want to bring your awareness to any destructive and unhealthy behaviors and habits that are interfering with your life purpose. At this time you need to make some healthy changes toward improving your health and well-being. You have been stuck in the same destructive patterns of behavior and habits for quite some time without doing anything constructive about them. This is due to a mixture of laziness, fear of change, and wishful thinking that your life will improve without any effort on your part. It is time for you to take charge and step up to the reality of your situation so that you can begin to turn things around. Ask the angels to help you, and you will allow a higher power to co-create in your desire to be healthy and balanced. Begin to evaluate the current path you are on, and eliminate everything that does not serve your greatest good. Addictions of all kinds, abusive relationships, bad habits, bad attitudes, and old limiting beliefs will all create psychic stress within your body and aura. This psychic stress will keep you firmly stuck, and patterns will continue to repeat themselves unless you make healthy changes. Finding a gray feather at this time suggests that now is your chance to do something about the areas of your life that are destructive.

Black Feathers

A black feather is not a sign that a dark angel (fallen angel) is near. The intuitive message of the black feather is that the angels want to help prepare you for some major life changes. Usually, from a place deep within you, you already know that change is coming because change is often needed. The intention of the angels is to help you and not to frighten you in any way. God will never give you more than you can handle in life, and He will send you His angels to help you in all your ways.

Life changes can be initially scary, can be emotionally painful at times, and can often make you feel as though the rug is being been pulled out quickly from under your feet. In other words, you can easily feel unbalanced as the world around you, which you routinely know and are comfortable with, begins to change. During this time you need to know that a higher power is fully aware of what is happening to you. The angels will surround you with Divine light and will continue to help guide you through any stumbles, emotional wobbles, and fearful moments you may experience until you regain your overall balance and well-being.

Finding a black feather can also signify that it is time for you to pay close attention to your darkened mind-set. The angels want to help support you in overcoming any destructive thoughts, beliefs, habits, and addictions that are causing you to sabotage your dreams, desires, health, and well-being. It is time to lean on a higher power to help you and to take responsibility to make positive, life-enhancing changes.

I will close this chapter by leaving you with a beautiful angel prayer that can help you feel safe and peaceful, trusting that a higher power is watching over you. I was taught to say this particular prayer in school as a very young child, and it is one that I still say today. I have felt a close connection to the angels throughout my life and I am certain that the power behind this prayer has kept me closely connected to the celestial realm:

> "Lord, keep us safe this night,
> secure from all our fears;
> may angels guard us while we sleep,
> till morning light appears."

> —John Leland, 1792

Chapter 4
How to Hear the Angels

When you are lonely or frightened, talk
to your guardian angel; you can do it out
loud or inside your head—your angel
can hear you.

—Joan Wester Anderson,
Where Angels Walk

Angels love to whisper their helpful guidance
to you. In this chapter you are going to learn how
to "spiritually hear" what the angels want to tell
you. The angels are happy to communicate with us
in this way, as it will help us deepen our spiritual
connection with them. Hearing the angels involves
more than just the physical aspect of hearing sounds;
the main way in which you will "hear" the majority
of angel messages are within your intuitive mind.

However, the angels can and will still utilize physical sounds to get our attention when needed. The
practical exercises in this chapter will help you to
fine-tune your energy frequency and develop your
clairaudient ability. Regular practice of these exercises will soon help you to sensitize your spiritual
hearing.

Clairaudience

Clair is a French term that translates as "clear."
Clairaudience, therefore, means "clear hearing." By
adjusting your energy frequency, which simply
means that you raise your vibration into an altered
meditative state, you will then be able to clear a
space within your intuitive mind through which you
can receive angelic information—which will enter
via your thought process. These thoughts come from
a spiritual source and not from your own thinking.
To begin with, the information you receive is often
delivered to you in a very subtle way, so much so
that you can easily feel as though you are making it
all up. This is because the message you receive will
still sound like *your own unique mental voice*. It is very
rare that you will hear otherworldly voices talking
to you inside your head. (Remember: the angels
will mostly use your own mental thought process to
reach you.) So, if this is what you are waiting to hear,

you will be waiting a very long time, and you will miss out on the loving, wise guidance of the angels.

There are certain times, however, when the angels will use a clear, loud physical voice to speak directly to you. Usually this happens in the case of an emergency—as an avenue for them to quickly deliver a helpful warning to you. This is known as *angelic intervention* or *Divine intervention*. There have been many reports from around the world of people hearing otherworldly voices, giving them clear and direct instructions that have helped save them from impending danger. These same people believed that the voice they heard was the intervention of their guardian angel at work in their lives. Angels do not have physical voices as we do because they are spiritual beings, so they will communicate to each other in a spiritual way. This can be likened to a mind-to-mind process or a telepathic connection. However, they can use a male or female voice if need be, and this is what you will "hear" when they speak directly to you.

When Angels Use Physical Sound to Speak to Us

* Angelic intervention.
* Hearing your name called upon awakening from sleep.

* High-pitched ringing noise in your ears.
* Celestial music.
* Other people's conversations.

Angelic Intervention

The angels will use the sound of a physical voice to deliver a warning to you to avoid any impending danger or harm, or to reveal an important piece of information to you. For example, a person may be be driving too fast and suddenly hear a clear and commanding voice giving him a direct instruction to "slow down." Someone may be walking toward possible harm and hear a loud and clear voice saying to "stop" or "turn around." You will intuitively know that the voice has your best interests at heart because of the way that it is delivered, and you will feel compelled to listen.

Hearing Your Name Called Upon Awakening From Sleep

Sometimes you may hear your name being called out to you upon awakening. This is because the angels know that it is much easier for you to hear them when you are in a highly relaxed state of consciousness, one that can be attained midway between being half-asleep and half-awake. This is a similar state to meditation, and meditation is one of the best ways to help you sensitize your inner hearing to the subtle frequency of the angels. The angels will often do this to let you know that they are working with you to help you develop your spiritual hearing.

High-Pitched Ringing Noise in Your Ears

On occasion you will hear a high-pitched ringing noise in your ears, either one or both, that lasts for a few seconds. The angels can use this high vibrational frequency as a channel to deliver pertinent information to you from a higher power; this information will usually concern specific knowledge about your life purpose. This information is being downloaded to you from the higher spiritual realm and will eventually filter through into your conscious awareness when you are ready to receive it, so you can begin to make certain progress in your life.

Celestial Music

Celestial music can help elevate your vibration, and it also has a wonderful healing effect on your physical body. Celestial music is energizing, uplifting, and revitalizing, and is a powerful healing tonic to our body, emotions, mind, and soul. Celestial music will often play during our sleep process. When we sleep, our bodies begin to naturally heal and revitalize, and celestial music will help to empower our nightly healing rejuvenation.

This sweet music is so powerful that it will often stay in your conscious mind upon awakening, and it can momentarily replay itself within your mental energy throughout the day. This is how you end up physically hearing it. How do you know that this music is angelic and from the celestial realms? Because when you hear it, you will not easily forget it. Celestial music can also be heard during meditation, or when you are immersed in and connected to nature. This suggests that an altered state of consciousness, *raising your vibration*, is required for you to first hear the music, but then it can fleetingly burst into your physical consciousness because it is so powerful. Ask your guardian angel to bring you the healing energy of celestial music while you are sleeping to help clear and energize your aura or to help uplift you when your spirits are low.

Other People's Conversations

You may overhear a conversation among other people and find that there will be some piece of relevant information within it for you. You don't even need to know the people to receive insight from them in this way. After all, it is the angels who are bringing you the message through the avenue of other people's voices. They already know how the conversation is going to play out, and all they need to do is to help place you exactly where you need to be in the hope that you will physically hear what you need to hear. Here's an example: You're sitting in a coffee shop and overhear two women at the next table discussing a workshop they are participating in. Your previous request to your guardian angel was to ask them to help you find the right workshop for you. Therefore, you need to take extra notice of the workshop they are talking about and then take some action to look it up. This, of course, is within your free will to do, but remember there are no coincidences—especially when you have already asked for help. Now let's take a look at spiritual hearing!

Angel Whispers—"Spiritual Hearing"

Because angels are spiritual beings, they like to communicate with us in spiritual ways, and typically they will do this by transferring, downloading, and placing their helpful guidance directly into our minds. The angels love to whisper their helpful guidance to us in the hope that we will be able to pay attention and listen. When developing clairaudience you will increase your ability to pay attention and listen to what the angels have to say. Angelic information that is delivered to us through our thoughts will usually have the accompanying intuitive feeling connected to it that you need to pay special attention to. For example, if you are pondering whether you should look for another job, your guardian angel may impress your thoughts with a certain person's name, and you will also have the accompanying intuitive feeling that you should tell that person about your desire. You listen to your guardian angel's guidance and you contact the person. You are then delighted to find out that he or she knows where there is a very good job opportunity for you. Guardian angels are aware of the best opportunities for you and will do their best to help guide you via the avenue of spiritual hearing, or as I like to call it, "angel whispers"!

What to Expect When the Angels Spiritually Talk to You

When the angels talk to you, you will find that you will rarely hear more than a whole sentence at a time unless you are lightly channeling information. Channeling information allows an angelic energy to place a natural flow of thoughts within your intuitive mind. (You will discover how to do this when you write a letter to your guardian angel later in this chapter.) What you will mostly experience when using clairaudience is usually a one- or two-word association of either symbolic or actual information, or a mixture of both. One or two words of symbolic information, when interpreted, can reveal a whole deeper meaning and insight for you. One or two words of actual information are more direct and not usually open to interpretation, as the information is literal. The following example includes how to interpret both actual and symbolic information so that you become aware of how you can gain a deeper insight into the messages that you will receive from the angels.

Let's pretend that you hear the word *orange* within your intuitive mind. The actual meaning would therefore be the fruit orange or the color orange. For the symbolic information, you will need to dig a little deeper and contemplate on what *orange* symbolizes in general, and also what it means to you personally. For example, the fruit orange can symbolically represent vitamin C, orange juice, or an orange tree, or it can represent *fruit* as a whole. This can therefore be interpreted that you may need to include fruit in your diet, or you may need some vitamin C as a tonic to help you strengthen your immune system. However, be sure to think about what *orange* symbolizes personally to you, as the angels will use information that is stored away in your chakras and aura, which is your memory bank and database of all of your personal information. They will do this to help stir your conscious awareness to the exact message they want you to hear.

Colors can offer you an even greater insight as they hold specific energetic frequencies and are also related to your chakras and aura. Here is a basic example about the color orange to show you how you can gain a greater perspective from just one color: The frequency of the color orange represents your creative energy. Maybe you want to join a drama group, a dance class, an art class, a writing class, a singing class, or a cooking class, but you have been putting it off. Developing your creativity will aid you in your connection with the angels. The color orange is also connected to your emotional health. Maybe you are blocking your emotions for fear of feeling your inner pain, and the angels want to help you free your emotions to regain your aura power. One specific color spoken within your intuitive mind can help to bring you significant insight and information. See Chapter 3 for information on the energy of color, found in the section about feathers. Also see Chapter 2 for information on the chakras, their associated colors, and their associated levels of consciousness.

How to Distinguish Between Real Angelic Information and False Guidance

* If you hear anything coming through that is not in alignment with Divine love, you can be sure that it will be your imagination doing the talking or some interference from

a low-level spirit giving you false guidance. Your guardian angel and all other angelic beings will always bring the feeling of love, support, joy, peace, and safety whenever they communicate with you. If you do feel fearful at any time, simply stop the connection and do the grounding exercise from Chapter 2. You have nothing to fear when the angels are near!

* Angels will never demand that you to do anything, especially anything destructive or harmful to yourself or others. Angels are loving, peaceful beings who honor your free will.

* False guidance (usually your ego) will attempt to continuously praise you. The angels will offer you a glimpse of your greatest potential, and encourage you to reach it, but not to the point where they always need to praise you.

Developing Clairaudience

Natural clairaudients are those people who are really good listeners. They will often work in the profession of care-givers, teachers, healers, and musicians. Natural clairaudients are also extra sensitive to noise. If you don't like loud noises, loud music, or living in a noisy environment, your heightened sensitivity could be a clue to your natural disposition of clairaudience. If noise doesn't bother you so much just now, you will soon find that when you begin to develop your clairaudient ability, you will become more sensitive to the noises around you.

A very natural way to help you develop clairaudience is for you to become aware of all the noises that you encounter on a daily basis. A good technique to use is to try to single out and tune into one specific form of noise at a time, while tuning out the rest. Focus on the birds singing, or the noise of the traffic, or a certain person's voice. When you do this, you are naturally sensitizing yourself to become clairaudient. Another way in which you can become sensitive to hearing is by spending regular time in silence without having any distractions from things such as the television, the phone, or the computer. The best way to do this is through the practice of daily meditation.

Meditation to Develop Clairaudience

Meditation is certainly one of the best ways to help you sensitize your spiritual hearing. The regular practice of meditation will help to calm your busy mind, raise your vibration, and clear your energy so that a space is made for you to receive clairaudient messages from the angels. The following quick and easy meditation, used daily, will help you specifically enhance and develop your clairaudient ability. This is my personal favorite meditation and one that I still use today. It was because of my daily use of this particular mediation over many years that I made finalist for "Best Female Medium" in the whole of Wales, UK, because it helped me to deeply sensitize my spiritual hearing.

✳ Use the white light of protection exercise. (See Chapter 2.)

✳ Close your eyes and focus on your breathing to help you relax. When you breathe in, imagine your aura expanding, and when you breathe out, allow any stress within you to leave. Do this several times and completely relax your body from your head to your toes. Mentally repeat the following affirmation three times: "I am deeply relaxed, safe, and happy." You have now prepared your energy frequency.

✳ Next, allow any thoughts you have to simply enter into your mind and then leave again without trying to focus on any of them. By doing this, you won't give your full attention to any problems or issues you are currently experiencing. (Your fears will often come to the surface when your mind is quiet, but you are going to let them float on by.)

* As you relax more, you may start to notice different colors beginning to form within your mind's eye. This is a very subtle process and nothing that is dramatic in any way. If you don't see these colors it doesn't matter, as the only task required of you is to relax. If you do see them, just pleasantly notice each color as it arrives and then changes into the next one. The whole purpose of this meditation is for you to sit in silence to help you sensitize your inner hearing. Nothing else is required of you—it is that easy—but at the same time it is also very powerful because when you do this meditation daily you are building aura power.

* Stay in this relaxed state for at least 10 to 20 minutes (building up to 30 minutes daily). When you feel you are ready to finish your meditation, simply bring your awareness back into the room. Feel the weight of your body on your chair, move your fingers

and toes, and then open your eyes. Have a drink of water and a light snack to help you ground your energy.

This next exercise is going to help you to spiritually hear the voice of your guardian angel talking to you within your intuitive mind.

Exercise:

How to Spiritually Hear Your Guardian Angel (Clairaudience)

✳ Use the white light of protection exercise. (See Chapter 2.)

✳ Close your eyes and settle yourself into a comfortable breathing rhythm. Begin by taking a few long and slow deep breaths in through your nose and out of your mouth; this will help to get the energy flowing in your body. When you breathe in, imagine the aura around you expanding, and when you breathe out, feel yourself relaxing more deeply. Do this several times.

✳ Open your chakras from the base to the crown by visualizing each one as spinning around in a clockwise direction (as if you were the face of the clock) and expanding. Use the color of each chakra to help you keep your focus strong: red, orange, yellow, green, turquoise blue, indigo, violet. This will only take a few minutes; it is helping you to prepare your entire aura vibration by allowing your energy to flow, expand, and energize.

✳ Next, send a mental intention to your guardian angel asking your angel to talk to you. Start the conversation off by asking a direct question, such as "What is your name?" Or ask your guardian angel to tell you what it looks like or to say something inspirational. Once you have asked the question, simply wait in a meditative relaxed state to help keep your energy vibration high. If you are desperate to hear from your guardian angel, your vibration will begin to drop and you will move out of range.

✳ Pay attention to any one or two words that you may subtly hear within your mind (remembering that they will sound like your own thoughts). For example, you may hear a specific name, or you may hear the word *believe* or *forgive*.

✳ Well done! You have just heard the voice of your guardian angel talk to you. The more that you acknowledge the subtle ways in which you hear the voice of your angel, then the stronger your clarity of spiritual hearing will become. Thank your guardian angel for its love, protection, and guidance.

✳ Now it's time to close down. Simply bring your awareness back into the room. Feel the weight of your body on your chair, move your fingers and toes, and open your eyes. Visualize intense white light pouring into your crown chakra and traveling through the central energy column until it reaches your base chakra. The white light will help to return your chakra frequencies back to their normal rates and sizes so that you will remain in a healthy, balanced state. This will only take a few minutes. Repeat the following affirmation: "I am grounded." Think about what you heard from your guardian angel, and write it down in your journal. Have a drink of water or a light snack to help ground your energy.

With practice and patience you will soon discern your guardian angel's voice in comparison to your own thoughts and imagination. Regular practice will also enable you to naturally increase your vibration so that you won't necessarily need to use this exercise to hear the voice of your angel. Over time it will become easier for you to automatically shift your awareness and frequency to the angel's frequency. Now we can move onto using clairaudience through the process of light trance channeling.

Channeling via Clairaudience

The angels can channel greater amounts of information and inspiration to you through the process of light channeling. To be able to channel information from the angels in this way you will first need to shift your awareness into an altered state of consciousness, also known as the *alpha state*. This is a very light form of trance and is equivalent to a meditative state or daydreaming. Channeled information can flow through your mind very quickly, so one of the best ways to gain full advantage of what you receive is to write it down as it flows to you. The following exercise will help you to lightly channel information in this way from your very own guardian angel in the form of an angel letter.

An Angel Letter

Writing a letter to your guardian angel will certainly help you to strengthen your communication with each other. The actual process of writing the letter will allow your intuitive mind the space it needs to clearly receive angelic guidance without any interference from your rational mind. This is because your conscious awareness is cleverly diverted by being focused on the physical act of writing, which then enables your intuitive mind to easily receive the spiritual guidance. You basically help yourself to get out of your own way so that your guardian angel can reach you.

An angel letter is a powerful technique that enables you to receive higher spiritual guidance, and even though it is you who is writing the letter and its reply, it is your guardian angel who will be gently influencing your thoughts during the reply. When it is time to write the reply, you will hear a steady flow of thoughts quickly streaming into your mind, and you will need to write them down without stopping its flow or without analyzing any of the information you receive. This is not the same technique as automatic writing, which occurs when a spiritual source takes control and direction of the pen. You are in control at all times.

To begin this exercise you first need to decide what it is that you would like to ask your guardian angel. Maybe you want to ask for guidance about a current issue you are having difficulty with. Once you have decided, you can begin to prepare your energy vibration to start the exercise. You will need a pen and paper.

Dear Guardian Angel...

☒ Use the white light of protection exercise. (See Chapter 2.)

☒ Close your eyes. When you breathe in, imagine your aura expanding, and when you breathe out, allow any stress you have within you to leave. Do this a few times and stay in a relaxed, meditative state for about five minutes to help you sensitize your energy vibration, which will place your brain waves in an alpha state.

☒ Send a strong mental intention to your guardian angel that you are going to write your guardian angel a letter. When you feel comfortable and ready, simply open your eyes and take hold of your pen and paper.

☒ Start by writing the words *Dear guardian angel,* and then continue to write exactly what it is that you want to say to your guardian angel. Be specific, and give as much detail as you can. Write in the same way as you would to your closest friend. During this time you may also want to ask your guardian angel to give you its name.

☒ Once you have finished the letter, sign it with your name, and then turn the page over to begin your reply. Your guardian angel is ready to answer you, and the moment you start writing your reply you will receive a steady flow of thoughts into your mind. Do not stop; keep writing until you feel you need to end the letter. Let's begin!

☒ Write down your own name as the reply heading: *Dear....*

☒ Now imagine that your guardian angel is answering your letter. Do not worry that you could be making it all up, as this will only serve to block the flow. Just focus on the act of writing, and write down what you spiritually hear. Do not try to make sense of what your angel is saying until you have finished the letter, or, again, you will block the natural flow.

☒ Once you have finished your letter, sign it from your guardian angel. Now read back what you have written. You will be amazed and surprised at the level of insight, wisdom, and inspiration that you have written on behalf of your very own guardian angel.

☒ Thank your guardian angel for guidance. Have a drink of water or a light snack to help ground your energy.

Chapter 5
Sensing the Angels

Insight is better than eyesight when it
comes to seeing an angel.

— *The Angels' Little Instruction Book*,
Eileen Elias Freeman, 1994

The angels want you to know that they are around
you and they can do this by merging their energy
vibration with your own so that you can begin to
sense and feel their angelic presence. You can register and feel both emotional sensations and physical
sensations in your aura and body when the angels
are near. Physical sensations can often include feeling a tickling sensation on your skin, feeling a tingling or slight buzzing vibration (mostly felt around
the head area), feeling body warmth, and feeling
an overall sensation of deep relaxation. Emotional

sensations can include an intuitive feeling that you just "know" that your angel is with you; you can also feel emotionally happy, uplifted, and inspired, and feel emotionally calm and supported by a higher power.

In this chapter, you will be given specific, practical exercises to help you develop your intuitive sensations to help you sense and physically feel the presence of your guardian angel around you. Regular practice of these exercises will help you fine-tune your intuition. The ability to sense the presence of the angels is known as *clairsentience*. Clairsentience is probably the most important spiritual ability to develop, as it enables you to have the power of discernment to be able to accurately discern unseen spiritual energies. Developing the power of discernment can also help you to intuitively choose the best course of action to take in your daily life through the use of your free will.

Clairsentience

Clair is a French term that translates as "clear." *Clairsentience*, therefore, means "clear sensing." This spiritual ability enables you to sense energy vibrations that emanate from angels, spirits, other people, and the environment. Developing your clairsentient ability will help you to become naturally sensitive to unseen energies, which is why it is important to protect your energy and to regularly do the energy-clearing exercise that you discovered in Chapter 2. "I sense; I feel" is what you will typically say and do when you are using your clairsentient ability.

You will also find that you will become more empathic and openhearted as a natural result of your development. The reason is that clairsentience is associated with the heart charka, and the heart chakra is associated with the love we have for humanity. The heart chakra is connected to the astral subtle energy body of our aura, the bridge between the higher spiritual dimensions and the material world. Therefore, when we develop our clairsentience, we will naturally help to sensitize our aura toward reaching higher spiritual vibrations so that we can begin to easily sense and feel the presence of angelic energy around us. Check through the following list of intuitive and physical feelings that will accompany an angelic presence around you so that you will know what to expect before you begin your development.

Emotional intuitive feelings that accompany an angelic presence:

- ✳ A feeling of Divine love.
- ✳ A happy, warm feeling inside.

* A safe, secure, and protected feeling.

* An uplifted feeling.

* A healing feeling (sensing you are receiving healing energy).

* A deep knowing that all will be well.

* A balanced and calm feeling.

* An emotionally supported feeling.

* Feeling faith, trust, and belief that your angel is near.

Physical feelings and sensations that accompany an angelic presence:

* Body heat.

* Relaxed feeling.

* Ruffling in your hair.

* Tickling on your face.

* Buzzing vibration around your head.

* Feeling a slight pushing or pressure sensation near you.

* Change in the air temperature around you.

* Feeling energized.

* Smelling the aroma of flowers around you.

* Reduced pain.

*F*alse Angelic Guidance

Now that you are aware of what to expect when you intuitively sense and physically feel the angels around you, the following information will reveal what to expect if you are receiving false angelic guidance. Low-level spirits and your own imagination can be the main culprits behind false guidance. If you have any of the following feelings and sensations when you connect to the angels, simply stop your connection and do the grounding exercise from Chapter 2. Remember, you are always in control.

Intuitive feelings indicating false guidance:

* Fear/uneasiness.

* Dislike of energy merging with yours (incompatible).

* Nervousness.

* Irritation.

* Angry thoughts.

* Feeling uncomfortable.

* Feeling that the connection does not serve your greatest good.

Physical feelings indicating false guidance:

* Fatigue.

* Nausea.

* Chills.

* Hair on your arms and back of your neck standing on end (goosebumps).

* Headache or migraine.

You will find that the negative impact of any physical feelings will immediately disperse when you detach yourself from the energy you are tuning into and when you do the energy-clearing exercise from Chapter 2. The more you pay attention to how you feel, the quicker you will be able to discern any negative energies so that you can easily deal with them.

Developing Clairsentience

Natural clairsentients are those people who have a very sensitive nature to other people's needs. They will be naturally compassionate, caring, and empathic, and the careers suited to these people often include medicine, nursing, energy healing, teaching, and all other vocations that require a caring nature. If you find that you become easily upset when you hear or see any disturbing news and then you can't shake it off because the feelings you have are so overwhelming, this is a sign that you are naturally clairsentient. If you can't help feeling sorry for everyone and from worrying about them incessantly, or from focusing on everyone's problems and thinking that you need to help fix them in some way, then you are naturally clairsentient. But you are also severely out of balance. Use the grounding exercise in Chapter 2 to help regain a healthy balance in your emotional health.

Listen to Your Heart

The best thing that you can do to help you naturally develop your clairsentient ability is to listen to your real, heart-based feelings. When you acknowledge the real feelings of your heart (this is not the same as your emotions, because emotions are fickle and can easily change), you will tap into your soul and connect to the divine direction for your life. Your real and true feelings are in alignment with your soul, higher-self, life purpose and God's will. If you listen to the truth within your heart, it will bring deep fulfillment and joy to your life. How do you start to listen to your real, heart-based feelings? You begin to monitor how you truthfully feel when you clearly focus in on all areas of your life, even if it is not what you want to feel. Blocking your heart energy for fear of getting hurt or fear of making changes will also block the flow of joy. Blocking your heart energy will also interfere with your clairsentient ability. You will naturally block your clairsentience when you are in direct conflict with your real, heart-based feelings. To discover how you *really* feel, ask yourself the following questions:

ıat am I ignoring for fear of change?

What am I blocking for fear of failure?

In what area of my life am I living a lie?

To help you develop and strengthen your clairsentient ability you need to clear the energetic blocks that interfere with your heart-based feelings. A very good way to connect with your heart-based feelings is to use the power of your imagination and your intuitive mind to *pretend* that you have already made certain changes. You can then check on how your heart really feels about them through any intuitive or physical sensations that you receive. For example, if you want to be free from your unhappy and unfulfilling relationship but are worried that you may make a big mistake if you do leave, then use your imagination to pretend that you have already left. Notice how this makes you feel. Do you feel happy and free, and know that you have made the right choice, or do you feel sad and full of regret? This process of using your imagination is very powerful, and it can usually help you resolve any conflicting emotions that get in the way of your real feelings. It can also help to ease your fears so you can begin to make significant and positive steps forward if need be. Keep your emotions in balance by honoring your emotional integrity and not doing anything that goes against your real heart-based feelings. When you listen to your heart you will naturally help to strengthen your clairsentience.

Sensing Energy

A powerful way to help you develop your clairsentient ability so you can sense and feel your guardian angel's energy is to use the art of *psychometry*, which simply means "to measure energy." The regular practice of psychometry will enable you to tune into and read the energy vibrations of people, objects, and places. When you practice this skill you will increase the sensitivity within your aura to easily sense and feel angelic energies. The easiest way to begin the practice of psychometry is to read the energy vibrations contained in a personal object of jewelry belonging to someone about whom you don't know too much. The personal object will be the energetic link that will help to connect you directly into that person's aura so that you can begin to feel and sense his or her energy vibrations.

For the following exercise you will need an item of jewelry from someone you do not know well and obviously the person's permission to do so. You can ask a friend if one of his or her friends would be willing to let you practice in this way, or maybe ask a coworker. The following exercise will help you sense energy vibrations from the object through easy, step-by-step instructions. The goal of this exercise is to help you develop your clairsentience to increase your sensitivity to the angels. Use a pen and paper to write down what you sense. Let's begin!

Psychometry Exercise:
Sensing Energy: "I Feel; I Sense"

✳ Use the white light of protection exercise. (See Chapter 2.)

✳ Close your eyes and settle yourself into a comfortable breathing rhythm. Begin by taking a few long and slow deep breaths in through your nose and out of your mouth; this will help to get the energy flowing in your body. When you breathe in, imagine the aura around you expanding, and when you breathe out, feel yourself relaxing more deeply. Do this several times.

✳ Open your chakras from the base to the crown by visualizing each one as spinning around in a clockwise direction (as if you are the face of the clock) and expanding. Use the color of each chakra to help you keep your focus strong: red, orange, yellow, green, turquoise blue, indigo, violet. This will only take a few minutes; it will help you prepare your entire aura vibration by allowing your energy to flow, expand, and energize.

✳ Set a mental intention that you are going to tune into this particular item of jewelry to retrieve information through your feelings and sensations. (This can also include feeling temporary physical sensations.)

✳ Hold the item of jewelry in either hand; it is a good idea to swap hands, as one hand can be more sensitive to energy than the other. (Usually it is the left one, but, over the years and from teaching many students this particular exercise, I have found either hand to work just as well.)

✳ Study the item of jewelry so that you place your focus and awareness there. To begin, all you need to do is to ask yourself the following question: How does this item of jewelry make me feel? Simply acknowledge any change in the way that you feel and write it down, even if it seems confusing. This will help keep the energy flowing with further information, as you can slow the process, or block more information from flowing when you do not consciously register your sensations.

✳ Next, use the following questions as a way to focus in on specific information to help you retrieve answers about the person who owns the jewelry.

❋ **Question:** What do this person's character and personality feel like? Example: You may suddenly feel happy, bubbly, calm, friendly, funny, serious, compassionate, moody, and so on. Simply acknowledge what you feel and write down what you receive.

❋ **Question:** What does this person's health feel like? Example: You may feel tired, energized, weak, strong, healthy, unhealthy; you may feel an area of temporary physical pain in your own body; or you may feel/sense a weakness in a particular area of your body.

❋ **Question:** What do I sense about this person's job? Example: You may get a sense that she works for herself; you may sense that she works with computers; you may sense that she is a nurse, a teacher, a mother, currently looking for a job, and so on.

❋ Now that you have a sense of how to focus in on specific information and the ways in which you may feel and sense energy vibrations, you may add your own questions into the mix to see what other vibes you can retrieve. You may also practice this exercise on different people to help you improve your accuracy.

❋ Now it's time to make an energy break and close down. Visualize intense white light pouring into your crown chakra and traveling through the central energy column until it reaches your base chakra. The white light is helping to return your chakra frequencies back to their normal rates and sizes so that your energy will remain in a healthy, balanced state. Say the affirmation "I am grounded." Have a drink of water or a light snack to help ground your energy. If you feel off-balance, use the grounding exercise in Chapter 2. Review what you have written and ask the person to indicate whether any of the information you have received about him or her is correct. This is a fun and easy way to strengthen your clairsentient ability. You can also use your clairsentient ability to sense the energy of people and places as follows.

———

Sensing People

You can easily feel energy vibrations emanating from people's auras. You will feel very comfortable with some people's energy, while other people can literally give you the creeps, which can send an energetic shiver running down your spine. People can lie, cheat, try to hide their real feelings, and pretend to be something they are not, but their energy frequency will always reveal the truth of their being. It is wise to always pay attention to how you feel when you meet someone for the first time.

You also need to be aware of how other people's energies make you feel when you are in close contact with them. If you work with clients in a physical or healing way, you can easily absorb any energetic pollution from your clients into your aura. This is why it is important to learn how to protect your energy and clear it regularly. Otherwise, a collection of other people's energies can begin to weigh you down; you will lose aura power and begin to feel exhausted and emotionally low. Use the following information as a guide to help retrieve the truth about a person's energy:

* When you meet someone for the first time, how does he make you feel? Do you trust his energy, or do you have a nervous or anxious feeling about him, even if he seems to be really friendly? If his energy feels familiar to you, then it will be a safe and trusting energy. If his energy feels strange to you or makes you feel uncomfortable, his energy will be incompatible to yours. This does not mean that there is anything wrong with him; it simply means that you do not resonate with each other on an energetic vibration. We all exist at

different levels of vibration, and, although opposites attract, you will feel more comfortable spending time with people who are on the same wavelength and vibration as you.

* When you spend time with certain people or when you work with certain clients, how do you feel afterward? Do you feel tired and drained? Do you feel tearful, irritable, angry, and not yourself? If so, you have absorbed energetic pollution, and you need to clear your energy.

Sensing Places

Places can absorb energy vibrations from past events that have occurred there, and these energy vibrations are amplified if what happened was especially traumatic. Old battlegrounds are a typical example of this due to all of the heightened emotions that were released there during the battle. Strong emotional reactions such as fear will be left behind in the atmosphere; this is known as *residual energy*. A sensitive person can feel this type of residual energy and tune into it to retrieve accurate information about the events that previously occurred there.

Whenever you visit somewhere new you can use your clairsentient ability to tune into the energy of the locale to discover if anything unusual has happened there. This is a fun exercise to do, especially if you are then able to do some research to check on the information you retrieved through your senses. Your feelings can be very accurate, and you may surprise yourself with what you pick up. Many people love to visit old castles, battlefields, and other areas where historic events took place. The following technique will help to activate your clairsentience to tune into any past events to retrieve information:

- ☒ Use the white light of protection exercise. (See Chapter 2.)

- ☒ Touch something solid such as a wall, a tree, or anything that can be associated with the past in the way of it being very old.

- ☒ Next, form a mental intention to tune into a time period of the past by stating, "I want to sense what happened here in this area more than 100 years ago" (or whatever time frame or specific date that you are drawn to). You can also allow your senses to go where they naturally take you by simply holding the desire to tune into the energy of the place.

- ☒ Next, begin to feel the energy change around you as you connect with past events. Use the following questions to activate your clairsentience:

* What do you sense/feel happened in this place?

* Do you sense/feel any strong traumatic energies, and if so, why?

* What time frame have you tuned into, how does this make you feel?

Sensing Your Own Energy

This simple technique will enable you to feel your *own energy vibration* so that you can feel something tangible and become aware of what energy feels like:

* Rub your palms vigorously together for a few minutes and then hold them several inches apart facing each other. Very slowly bring your palms toward each other until you feel some kind of resistance. When you feel resistance, you are connecting with your own energy.

Angelic Energies

Clairsentience will enable you to feel what your guardian angel and other angelic beings' energies feel like. Angels have different energies depending on their rank and their area of expertise. Some angels will have energy that feels soft and gentle to you, and this will be a clue that they are more feminine in nature. Other angels will have energy that feels strong and powerful, which will also be a clue that they are more masculine in nature. Your guardian angel's energy can feel caring, safe, and unconditionally loving. It will also feel more familiar and comfortable to you because it has always been with you. The Archangels' energies can feel more powerful because they exude a mighty presence. Angels are highly evolved spiritual beings, and their energies will always reflect this. When you are in the company of many angels you may feel extremely joyful, uplifted, and inspired.

The following will help you to sense and feel the presence of your very own guardian angel.

How to Sense and Feel the Energy of Your Guardian Angel

- ☒ Use the white light of protection exercise. (See Chapter 2.)

- ☒ Close your eyes and settle yourself into a comfortable breathing rhythm. Begin by taking a few long and slow deep breaths in through your nose and out of your mouth. This will help to get the energy flowing in your body. When you breathe in, imagine the aura around you expanding, and when you breathe out, feel yourself relaxing more deeply. Do this several times.

☒ Open your chakras from the base to the crown by visualizing each one as spinning around in a clockwise direction (as if you were the face of the clock) and expanding. Use the color of each chakra to help you keep your focus strong: red, orange, yellow, green, turquoise blue, indigo, violet. This will only take a few minutes; it will help you prepare your entire aura vibration by allowing your energy to flow, expand, and energize.

☒ Next, send a mental intention to your guardian angel stating that you would like to be able to sense and feel its energy around you.

☒ Now, mentally invite your guardian angel to step into your aura vibration and ask your guardian angel to place its wings around you. Take notice to see if you have any internal or external sensations and feelings. For instance, do you sense/feel any physical change in temperature within the space around you? Do you sense/ feel any sensations of gentle pressure pushing lightly against you? If you don't feel any physical sensations whatsoever, then you may feel internal sensations such as instantaneous joy, inner peace, or a lovely, safe, and protected feeling.

☒ Ask your guardian angel to tickle an area of your face; this can be your cheek, your nose, your forehead, or your chin. You can also ask your guardian angel to play with your hair. This can feel like a very light and gentle movement or a slight tickling of the scalp. What else do you feel? Other feelings and sensations can include a light buzzing or vibrating around your head, an internal feeling of gratitude, and an overall warm sensation encompassing your body.

☒ Well done! You have just felt the loving energy and touch of your very own guardian angel. The more that you acknowledge the subtle ways in which you sense and feel the energy of your guardian angel, the stronger your intuitive feelings and sensations will become. Thank your guardian angel for its love, protection, and guidance.

☒ Now it's time to close down. Simply bring your awareness back into the room. Feel the weight of your body on your chair, move your fingers and toes, and open your eyes. Visualize intense white light pouring into your crown chakra and traveling through the central energy column until it reaches your base chakra. The white light is helping to return your chakra frequencies back to their normal rates and sizes so that your energy will remain in a healthy, balanced state. Say the following affirmation: "I am grounded." Have a drink of water or a light snack to help ground your energy.

Chapter 6
How to See the Angels

Do not forget to entertain strangers,
for by so doing some people have
entertained angels without knowing it.

—Hebrews 13:2 (NIV)

In this chapter you are going to discover how to spiritually "see" the angels. It is very rare that you will get a chance to actually see an angel unless God decides otherwise and based on your need. Angels will sometimes manifest in physical form to help fulfill a specific purpose or to intervene in some way, but always under the will of God. So it is possible for an angel to cross your path in some way without you being fully aware of who the angel really is. However, it is possible for you to catch very quick glimpses of angelic energies around you with your physical vision that only last for a few seconds, if that. They appear to our physical eyes as dancing sparkles of colored light or white light, or as shooting orbs of light. The moment you try to focus on them they will disappear from sight. Angels love to give us physical signs of their presence in the hope that we will notice they are near.

Angels, as you know, are spiritual beings, and so the main way in which they will reach you will be through spiritual means. For you to be able to *see the angels,* you will need to activate and develop the spiritual sense of clairvoyance. Clairvoyance is the ability to use extrasensory perception to gain clear insight through visual mental pictures. A person said to have the ability of clairvoyance is referred to as a *clairvoyant.* The practical exercises in this chapter will help you to develop and activate your clairvoyant ability. You will then be able to use your clairvoyant vision to see your very own guardian angel.

Clairvoyance

Clair is a French term that translates as "clear." *Clairvoyance,* therefore, means "clear vision." You do not see with your physical eyes; you see with your inner vision, what is known as your mind's eye. The third eye chakra is the energy center that is associated with clairvoyance. The location of this energy center is found between the eyebrows in the center of the forehead and within our etheric subtle body. When the third eye chakra is activated, images and visions will appear there to be interpreted. These images and visions can be symbolic or literal in nature, so there is a need to interpret the symbolic visions you receive to get a clue as to what the real message and meaning are. The angels can use the avenue of your clairvoyant vision to deliver helpful guidance and insightful messages to you.

Some people have clairvoyant dreams, also known as precognitive dreams, which occur when you receive premonitions of possible future events within the dream state. Clairvoyance can also be used to predict the probable future and can be naturally activated when using divination tools such as angel oracle cards. People who are naturally clairvoyant are very aware of their surroundings; they easily notice and see the finer details around them that others tend to miss. They are visionaries, have good imaginations, and are drawn toward creative endeavors such as drawing, painting, writing, and storytelling. Natural clairvoyants find it easy to daydream and also dream a lot during their sleep. The following guidelines can help you to develop your natural clairvoyant ability:

* Practice living in the present moment so that your focus is not stuck in the past or ahead into the future.

* Learn to observe your surroundings, noticing as many small things as you can around you.

* Let your imagination run free by writing stories that include wonderful characters and adventures.

* Join an art class to help you find your creative inspiration and to tap into your imagination.

* Single out a certain model and color of car, and then notice how many times you see it throughout the day. You will be surprised at the results.

* Use angel cards to help you awaken your inner vision.

How to Distinguish Between Real Angelic Visions and False Visions

Check through the following list of real and false angelic visions. False angelic visions will often come from the interference of your own imagination or low-level spirits.

Real physical angelic visions (lasting for seconds):

* Sparkles of colored light, white light, and orbs of light.

* Translucent shimmering light energies in the shape of an angel.

* Colored or white mists of light.

* Clouds formed in the shape of an angel (an immediate visual sign that your angel is near).

Real spiritual angelic visions (seeing in your mental energy with your eyes opened or closed, also lasting seconds):

* Seeing a mental picture of a beautiful angel with wings in an aura of light.

* Seeing a mental picture of a human with white robes or dressed in an aura of light.

* Seeing a mental vision of colored lights or colored mists.

* Seeing a mental vision of an angel of light closely connected to another person.

* Seeing a mental vision of an angelic-looking face.

* Seeing a mental picture of white feathers.

False angelic visions:

* A frightening vision of an angel being.

* A vision that lacks an aura of light energies (possible low-level spirits).

* A vision that doesn't intuitively feel right. (You will also be using clairsentience here.)

* A vision that offers angelic guidance that doesn't intuitively sound correct. (You will also be utilizing clairaudience here.)

Always check in with how you feel and what you "hear" whenever you receive any visions. You are developing the power of discernment and you will easily be able to distinguish between false angelic visions and real angelic visions when you use all of your spiritual senses. For one thing, low-level spirits may be able to pretend to be someone they are not, but their energy will always reveal the truth about them. They will not hold enough Divine light within their aura to shine brightly, so you will be able to see, sense, and hear that they are not in alignment with Divine love. Low-level spirits cannot fool you, as you have more Divine light within you than they have within them. Remember, you are always in control. You have nothing to fear when the angels are near!

Developing Clairvoyance

Developing clairvoyance will enable you to intuitively see your guardian angel and other angelic beings. Your guardian angel can also deliver insightful guidance to you via your inner vision. You can ask your angel to show you information that is beneficial to you. For example, if you have misplaced your car keys, you can ask your guardian angel to help you find them by giving you a mental vision of where they are. Remember that images and visions can be symbolic or literal in nature. As a quick example, if you receive an image of a boat on calm waters, the actual image will be a boat (you may be about to go on a cruise or a boat trip). The symbolic interpretation of a boat on calm waters can mean that a stressful situation you have currently been going through is about to calm down and smooth out for you. The following exercise will help you to develop your clairvoyant ability.

Exercise:
The Clairvoyant Screen

Every thought and emotion that we have ever had, all knowledge and wisdom that we have acquired throughout this lifetime, including all of our past lives, will be stored as data within our unconscious mind. Whenever we use our clairvoyant ability an image will be selected from our stored database of knowledge held within us and brought into the forefront of our mind's eye. Our guardian angel can also transfer information into our minds when we ask a direct question. For this exercise you will need to have a friend hide your car keys or your cell phone within your own home. Then you can ask your guardian angel to show you where you can find them.

* Use the white light of protection exercise. (See Chapter 2.)

* Center your awareness in the area of your third eye chakra located in the center of your forehead. Imagine turning on a light switch from within your mind's eye, and the light then shooting out of your third eye chakra.

* Next, close your eyes and imagine a blank screen, just like one you would find at the movie theater, or create a blank wall or a television screen (whatever is easiest for you). This blank canvas is going to be the space where you will receive clairvoyant images. Any visions, glimpses, and images you receive can be extremely fast and fleeting, or can be clearer and last longer.

* Whenever you ask a question within your mind, an image or vision should appear on

your screen that is either actual or symbolic, and you will then need to work it out. If you do not understand the image you can always ask for more help to decipher it; you will then receive further images to help you.

✳ You can gain very accurate information and insight with the practice of this clairvoyant technique. Let's begin!

✳ Create your blank screen within your mind.

✳ Make the following request to help attract visual images from your unconscious mind to appear on your blank screen: "Dear angel, please show me where my car keys are."

✳ Wait for an image to appear. (You will probably receive an accurate image other than a symbolic image.) You may get an image of a certain room in your home, and your keys will be located somewhere within that room. Go into that room and as you scan the room, ask your angel to show you where you need to look. This time your guardian angel will transfer further images into your mind's eye to reveal the exact location; or your guardian angel will direct your physical vision to look in a certain place. This is such a fun exercise to do, and the more fun you have, the more power your aura will have to help activate your clairvoyant vision.

✳ Close down by turning off the "light switch." Thank your guardian angel for helping you, and have a drink of water or a light snack to help ground your energy.

———

Spiritual Vision (Seeing Angels)

Angels can physically appear to us for reasons such as Divine intervention, when they are able to materialize and intervene in our lives in times of possible danger. The mysterious stranger is there at just the right moment to offer his or her help, but suddenly disappears before you are able to thank him or her. Angels will also physically appear to people when they are about to cross over to the spirit world. People on the verge of dying have spoken of angel beings or spirit loved ones waiting for them to go with them. Other people in the room cannot see what the dying person can see because his or her energy is much heavier and grounded.

Other reports of people seeing angels occur when people have had a near-death experience. They will accompany the soul of the person on a tour of the afterlife, revealing spiritual wisdom and insight into the person's life on Earth. People and children who have experienced angels in this way have described them as very tall, glorious beings of light.

Angels are usually invisible to us because their energy frequency is vibrating extremely quickly, whereas our energy frequency is much slower. The difference between our frequencies is what makes it difficult for us to see them with our physical eyes. To give you an example of this, think of a ceiling fan that has two speeds, one slow and one fast. You will still see the individual fan blades when they rotate at the slow speed, but if you speed up the fan, the individual blades blur into one, and you won't see them anymore. The main way in which we will spiritually see angels is therefore within our dreams and within our meditations.

The following exercise is a guided visualization meditation to meet with your guardian angel. It will help to activate your inner vision through the power of your imagination.

Exercise:
Meditation to See Your Guardian Angel

❋ Use the white light of protection exercise. (See Chapter 2.)

❋ Close your eyes and settle yourself into a comfortable breathing rhythm. Begin by taking a few long and slow deep breaths in through your nose and out of your mouth, as this will help to get the energy flowing in your body.

When you breathe in, imagine the aura around you expanding, and when you breathe out, feel yourself relaxing more deeply. Do this several times.

✳ Open your chakras from the base to the crown by visualizing each one as spinning around in a clockwise direction (as if you were the face of the clock) and expanding. Use the color of each chakra to help keep your focus strong: red, orange, yellow, green, turquoise blue, indigo, violet. You have now prepared your energy frequency.

✳ Mentally invite your guardian angel to meet with you, stating that you would like to see what your guardian angel looks like. Let's begin!

✳ Imagine that you are within your own home, as this will help you to feel safe and secure. When you feel ready, open your door and you will notice the most beautiful garden you have ever seen. Step into the garden and close the door behind you. You see a pathway and you begin to walk along it. Everywhere you look is the most beautiful scenery. The day is glorious, the sun is shining, the birds are singing, and there are pretty butterflies all around you. Soon you notice a beautiful white bench that is shaded from the sun by a great big oak tree.

✳ Take a seat on this bench and admire the beauty that surrounds you. What do you see? You feel safe, happy, and at peace sitting on your bench, and you are totally in the moment. Soon you begin to feel excitement start to build inside you as you are aware that your guardian angel is about to join you. You feel a gentle breeze brushing past you and you know it is a sign that your angel has arrived.

✳ Glance to your side and you will see that your guardian angel has come to join you by sitting with you on the bench. You can easily see your angel and you are mesmerized by this magnificent angelic being of light. What does your angel look like? You are going to remember as much detail from this meditation as you can. Notice whether your guardian angel has any wings. If so, what color are they? Do you have a male or female angel? Gather as much visual information as you can so that you can remember later on.

✳ You now discover that your guardian angel has a special gift for you. You lovingly accept this gift and then open it to find out what it is. You may feel as though you are making it all up, but ignore this feeling and just go with the flow of your imagination. Make sure you remember the gift your guardian angel gave you so that when you come back from your meditation, you can use your intuition to interpret what you have been given.

✳ Thank your guardian angel for the gift and for visiting with you. Say goodbye, and then find the path and begin to make your way back home. Open the door and step into your home, and then close the door behind you.

✳ Now it's time to close down. Simply bring your awareness back into the room. Feel the weight of your body on your chair, move your fingers and toes, and open your eyes. Visualize intense white light pouring into your crown chakra and traveling through the central energy column until it reaches your base chakra. The white light will help to return your chakra frequencies back to their normal rates and sizes so that you will remain in a healthy, balanced state. Repeat the following affirmation: "I am grounded." Have a drink of water or a light snack to help ground your energy. Write down everything you remember about your mediation. Use your intuition to interpret the symbolic gift you received from your guardian angel.

Examples of Gifts You May Receive, With Their Intuitive Messages

✳ A golden pen: You need to write inspirational ideas, poems, work on a book, or keep a journal. Your guardian angel wants to inspire you to write.

✳ An apple: You may need to pay attention to your diet and improve the quality of what you eat by adding in fresh fruit and vegetables. This will help you to elevate your energy frequency.

✳ A crystal: What crystal is it? A rose quartz can help you to heal a broken heart. An amethyst crystal can help to protect you. A clear quartz crystal can help you with clairvoyant vision. You may be guided to go on a crystal healing workshop.

✳ A golden book: Knowledge and wisdom will come to you from books, teachers, and workshops. You are about to enter a period of study and contemplation.

✳ A feather: What color is the feather? The message can represent the color interpretation of the feather. (See Chapter 3.) Your guardian angel is giving you a simple and clear sign that it is with you.

✳ A star: You need to raise your expectations
   and let your soul shine brightly in all that
   you do. You are going to receive an award,
   good news or some kind of celebration.

———

I will close this chapter with a beautiful guardian
angel prayer:

> Angel of God, my guardian dear,
> to whom God's love commits me here;
>
> Ever this day, be at my side,
> to light and guard, to rule and guide.

— Old English Prayer

Chapter 7
Heaven's Mighty Seven: The Archangels

How the mighty and powerful Archangels can help you within your life!

Heaven's seven mighty and powerful Archangels have special qualities and tasks given to them by God to help serve humankind. There are, however, many more than seven Archangels, but this chapter is going to focus on seven specific Archangels who have powerful energies that can assist you within your daily life. These magnificent Archangels are ranked higher than the guardian angels in the celestial hierarchy, although they do still belong to the same angelic choir. Archangels hold a strong and mighty presence within the spiritual realm, and their Divine role is to carry out the will of God, helping to serve humankind and the universe.

The Archangels Michael, Gabriel, and Raphael are probably the best-known of the seven Archangels. Archangel Michael is the chief Archangel who leads the heavenly armies in battle with Satan. The Archangel Gabriel is God's important messenger who delivered the news to Mary that she would give birth to the baby Jesus. (The angel said to her, "Do not be afraid, Mary; you have found favor with God. You will conceive and give birth to a son, and you are to call him Jesus. He will be great and will be called the Son of the Most High. The Lord God will give him the throne of his father David, and he will reign over Jacob's descendants forever; his kingdom will never end." [Luke 1:30–33 (NIV)])

The Archangel Raphael is mentioned by name in the Book of Tobit as one of the seven who stand before the Lord. This mighty Archangel has special healing powers.

The other four Archangels who belong in this mighty group are considered to be the Archangels Jophiel, Chamuel, Uriel, and Zadkiel. Each one of the seven archangels has its own powerful ray of light energy bestowed on that Archangel by God to help serve humanity and the universe. The seven energy rays hold very high frequencies of Divine light, with each one representing a different aspect of God. The Archangels radiate their rays of Divine light to the world to help elevate the consciousness of humankind away from fear and destruction, and toward Divine love and peace. Each one of the seven rays has its own specific color energy frequency.

The Seven Spiritual Rays of Divine Light

* Archangel Michael serves on the first ray, which is the blue ray of Divine light, the energy frequency of God's will, protection, faith, and power.

* Archangel Jophiel serves on the second ray, which is the golden yellow ray of Divine light, the energy frequency of illumination, wisdom, and enlightenment.

* Archangel Chamuel serves on the third ray, the rose pink ray of Divine light and the energy frequency of Divine love.

* Archangel Gabriel serves on the fourth ray, the white ray of Divine light and the energy frequency of purity.

* Archangel Raphael serves on the fifth ray, the emerald green ray of Divine light and the energy frequency of Divine healing.

* Archangel Uriel serves on the sixth ray, the purple and gold rays of Divine light, is the energy frequency of peace.

* Archangel Zadkiel serves on the seventh ray, the violet ray of Divine light, and the energy frequency of freedom, mercy, and forgiveness.

Nearly all of the Archangels names end in "-el," meaning "in God," with the beginning of their names representing what each individual Archangel specializes in. The Archangels also have twin flames, which are their feminine counterparts, called *Archeia.* Archangels and their Archeia are able to help you with any problem that you have, but they cannot interfere with your karma, your spiritual lessons, or your free will. Again, you must ask them for their help. First read about each of the seven Archangels, and then find examples of questions that you can ask them to help you with.

Archangel Michael

Archangel Michael is probably the best-known Archangel. His name means "he who is like God." He is a mighty leader in charge of the Archangels and angels, and his energy is very strong, powerful, and protective. Often known as "Prince of the Angels," Archangel Michael is a force to be reckoned with. This mighty Archangel's twin flame is called "Faith," and together they serve on the first ray, which is the blue ray of God's power, will, faith, and protection. Archangel Michael is a warrior angel and is depicted in renaissance art as carrying a sword and shield ready for battle. He is the defender of the heavenly realms and he has legions of angels working with him on the blue ray of God's Divine light; together they help to disperse all negative energy and fear in the lower astral realms.

Archangel Michael works to change, heal, repair, and disperse everything within the universe and on the Earth that is not in alignment with God's will of Divine truth. The energy of fear moves us further away from Divine truth. Archangel Michael will help to remove the toxic energy of fear from our hearts and minds so that we can begin to remember who we really are—a Divine spark of God. Archangel Michael will help you to align your will with the will of God so that you can co-create your life with a higher power and fulfill your life purpose. Archangel Michael works to magnify God's power throughout the universe, and his Archeia, Faith, helps us to develop faith in God's power. With a deep faith in God we will become spiritually strong, igniting our belief that God will provide all of our needs and desires, will protect us in our lives, and will work miracles in our lives when needed. When we have faith in God's power we will also become courageous and strong in our own lives.

Archangel Michael can offer you both physical and spiritual protection if needed. Physical protection includes protecting you from the harmful intentions of others, protecting you from crime, protecting your property and possessions, and protecting you from accidents. Spiritual protection includes protecting your energy vibration and home environment from things such as interfering low-level spirits, demons, psychic attack, and other forms of negative energies that can weaken you. Archangel Michael will release all trapped, earthbound spirits to the light, along with all low-level spirits who are meddling and causing havoc in people's lives. He will also use his flaming sword of intense blue and white light to destroy any negative attachments you may have in your life, such as addictions, and cut away any negative psychic cords attached into your energy vibration by others.

The following exercise will help you to receive the protective energy of Archangel Michael. This is a powerful technique that will help to shield your aura from all forms of low-level spirits, psychic attack, and energetic stress caused by all kinds of negative energies. You can use it anytime you feel vulnerable or fearful, or whenever you feel the need to protect yourself. This technique involves visualization and physical interaction combined.

Exercise:
A Blue Cloak of Spiritual Protection

* Mentally ask for the protective energy of Archangel Michael to surround and protect your body and aura.

* Visualize a deep blue cloak of spiritual protection being placed over your shoulders. This magnificent blue cloak reaches all the way down past your feet and also has a very large hood. Imagine pulling the hood over your head. The blue cloak also has a zipper that travels from your base chakra to the crown chakra at the top of your head.

* Do the physical action of pretending to pull the zipper up of the imaginary cloak from your base chakra to the crown of your head. Hold your finger and thumb close to your body just as you would if you were really zipping up a coat. When you use a physical action along with your visualization, it will become more powerful for you, and you will begin to form a habit of

protection every time you zip up. This is a great and easy technique to teach your children.

✳ Your energy vibration will now have the protective force of Archangel Michael surrounding it. Thank God and Archangel Michael for your protection. You can use the following affirmation throughout the day to anchor your protection: "Divine love protects me."

———

The following questions are examples of what you can ask Archangel Michael to help you with. Simply form a clear, focused mental intention requesting his help, and be as specific as you can with your request; or, use the questions that are suggested. This process will activate spiritual power to work for you for your greatest good.

Dear Archangel Michael:

✳ Please can you protect me during my journey from all forms of danger and negativity?

✳ Please can you protect my loved ones, and help to keep them safe from all harm and danger?

✳ Please can you protect my home, car, and possessions from all harmful intentions?

* Please can you empower me with the courage to face what needs to be faced, or to do what needs to be done?

* Please can you help me to surrender and align my will with the will of God for my life?

* Please can you use your blue sword of light to cut and dissolve the negative psychic cords of energy that keep me attached to my addiction of (be specific), or to a destructive relationship with (say the person's full name) that I find too difficult to break away from on my own?

* Please can you use your blue sword of light to put an immediate stop to any psychic attack already in its tracks and to cut away any negative psychic cords of energy that already exist in my aura connected there by other people?

* Please can you clear my home of all low-level spirits or earthbound spirits, and the effects of any fear or negativity held within my home environment?

* Please can you help to free my heart and mind from the fear that is keeping me

from living in alignment with Divine truth?

✳ Please can you help me to strengthen my faith?

Archangel Jophiel

Archangel Jophiel's name translates as "beauty of God." He is a very beautiful Archangel who has an inspiring, uplifting, and joyful energy. You can feel emotionally and mentally elevated when this wonderful Archangel is near you. Archangel Jophiel and his Archeia, Christine, both serve on the second ray of God's Divine light, the golden yellow ray, helping to shine God's wisdom and illumination to the world. With God's wisdom of Divine truth we can begin to see things in a new light and can then move forward in our lives in an enlightened manner that will add much beauty to our planet. Archangel Jophiel can help illuminate our mental energy with beautiful ideas, which can reveal our unique gifts and talents so that we can use our creative energy to add our own beautiful expression into the world.

Archangel Jophiel can help us to see and appreciate the beauty in our own life and the world around us, especially when we are feeling emotionally low and we have lost the light within our soul. He can help inspire our mind with beautiful thoughts so that we will think about and perceive things in a more positive light, and he can help us to see the beauty in others rather than focusing on their faults. Archangel Jophiel and Christine will help us in our spiritual growth and development, giving us the spiritual insight we need and bringing us the spiritual knowledge we seek so that we can further enlighten our souls through reaching ever-higher levels of spiritual maturity. Together they help to bring spiritual wisdom and understanding to our lives. Both Jophiel and Christine take a great interest in helping us to increase our knowledge and wisdom. They will help students, teachers, and anyone who is open to expanding his or her knowledge and wisdom. They love to inspire us all to tap into our creativity, but they especially love to inspire artists to create beautiful works of art that can help enrich and beautify people's lives.

The following questions are examples of what you can ask Archangel Jophiel to help you with. Simply form a clear, focused mental intention requesting his help, and be as specific as you can be with your request; or, use the questions that are suggested. This process will activate spiritual power to work for you for your greatest good.

Dear Archangel Jophiel:

* Please can you enlighten me with knowledge about my life purpose?

* Please can you give me wisdom and clarity in this matter?
  (Say what it is.)

* Please can you help me to absorb knowledge and to remember it?

* Please can you help me to have clear focus through my studies and exams?

* Please can you help me to heal my mental energy of my negative thoughts?

* Please can you help me to discover the beauty within my own self and life?

* Please can you help me to develop spiritual intelligence?

* Please can you help to inspire me with a solution to this problem?
  (Say what it is.)

* Please can you help to inspire me to use my creative energy?

* Please can you help me to see this thing (say what it is) in a new light and perspective?

*A*rchangel Chamuel

Archangel Chamuel's name translates as "he who sees God." He is a very strong and beautiful Archangel who carries the energy of Divine love. You may feel more loving and compassionate when this wonderful Archangel is near you. Archangel Chamuel and his Archeia, Charity, both serve on the third ray of God's Divine light, the rose pink ray, helping to shine God's love to the world. God's Divine love is the source of all healing and is therefore the most important energy frequency throughout the entire universe.

> Only love is real; everything else is an illusion.
>
> *— A Course in Miracles*

God is love, and there is only one true power, which is the power of God's love. Anything else that exists in opposition to Divine love is therefore not real and has no real power over you, because remember — there is only one real power!

Archangel Chamuel and Charity are in charge of bringing Divine love to our planet and they will do what they can to help keep the peace. They will use the pink ray of Divine love to dissolve the low vibrational energies of hatred, as well as all other fearful and negative energies that are created by mass consciousness and that linger like one big, black cloud in our atmosphere, so that the Divine love of God can shine through and be revealed.

This mighty Archangel is concerned with the love we have for humanity. He will help us discover the Divine spark of love we hold within us so we can ignite this spark to help serve each other in unconditional, loving, and selfless ways. God's Divine spark of love exists in each and every one of us; therefore we are all an individual part of the one true source of power, which is God. It is the belief that we are separate from God and from each other that causes so many problems within our lives and within our world.

On a more personal level, Archangel Chamuel and Charity can help us to unconditionally love and accept ourselves, and to connect with our true self. They will help us heal and overcome any depression or self-hatred that has taken hold of us. They will also help us with any issues of un-forgiveness, free us from any guilt we carry, help us improve our destructive behaviors that are the opposite of love, and help us use our creative energy as an expression of love. When we express lovingkindness to others we will help magnify God's Divine love to the world.

Archangel Chamuel and Charity can help us develop the spiritual qualities that are associated with unconditional love: patience, tolerance, and kindness. They especially like to help us heal and mend our relationships with others, such as family disputes, or any arguments and disagreements that we have with others. They will also help us heal when we are heartbroken due to our overwhelming grief from losing a loved one, or due to a relationship breakup. Archangel Chamuel can help you *open your heart* to find your soul mate and bring love into all areas of your life. He can also help you increase your gratitude for the love you already have so that you do not take it for granted.

When you examine all areas of your life to discover what no longer fulfills you, Archangel Chamuel is happy to help you find more fulfilling, loving, and joyful ways for you to live. This can include a new job, a new career, a new relationship, or just a new and healthy daily routine. Archangel Chamuel is very good at finding things. All you need to do, of course, is ask!

The following questions are examples of what you can ask Archangel Chamuel to help you with. Simply form a clear, focused mental intention requesting his help, and be as specific as you can be with your request; or, use the questions that are suggested. This process will activate spiritual power to work for you for your greatest good.

Dear Archangel Chamuel:

* Please can you help me to mend my broken heart?

* Please can you help me to forgive myself and others? (Be specific with your issue.)

* Please can you help me to love and accept myself?

* Please can you help me to develop the spiritual qualities of unconditional love?

* Please can you help me to resolve my family dispute?

* Please can you help me to heal and repair my relationship with (say the person's name)?

* Please can you help me to develop patience, tolerance, and understanding?

* Please can you help me to express my creativity and find joy in my work?

* Please can you help me to appreciate the love that I already have in my life?

* Please can you help me to find a romantic soul mate relationship?

* Please can you help me find my lost item? (Be specific.)

* Please can you help me to find inner peace?

Archangel Gabriel

Archangel Gabriel's name translates as "God is my strength." This glorious Archangel's Archeia is named Hope, and together they serve on the fourth ray of God's Divine light, the white ray, helping to shine the energy of God's purity to the world. The energy frequency of God's brilliant white light can help clear all energetic contamination from the world that is impure and is not in agreement with God's Divine truth. On a more personal level, Archangel Gabriel and Hope can help clear all energetic contamination from your body, mind, soul, and life that interferes with who you really are. If you are moving away from God's light into the murky shadows of darkness, Archangel Gabriel can help clear the muck so that you can begin to purify your life to live in peace and harmony.

Archangel Gabriel and Hope will bring you the strength, hope, and encouragement you need to help you break free from any difficulties you are struggling with, such as addictions or temptations. They can also help you keep a clear conscience so that you do not have any guilt weighing heavily on your mind. When you are pure of heart and mind, you have integrity, you will serve others with love, you are free to experience peace of mind, and you will align your spirit with God's truth.

Archangel Gabriel is by far the best-known messenger angel and is often depicted as carrying a trumpet ready to announce good news. This mighty Archangel delivered the news to Mary that she would be pregnant with and give birth to the baby Jesus. Archangel Gabriel can also bring us news about our own spiritual life purpose, and can deliver helpful spiritual guidance to us that will enable us to fulfill our life path and spiritually progress. As an important messenger angel, Archangel Gabriel can help us acknowledge the many signs and messages that are all around us from a higher power and are answers to our internal questioning.

Archangel Gabriel can help you to communicate your truth in a peaceful and loving manner. He will work with all God's spiritual messengers on Earth to help them clearly communicate God's Divine truth and love. Archangel Gabriel and Hope can also give inner strength and hope to discouraged parents who are having difficulty conceiving or adopting a child. As always, all you need to do is to ask!

The following questions are examples of what you can ask Archangel Gabriel to help you with. Simply form a clear focused mental intention requesting his help, and be as specific as you can be with your request; or, use the questions that are suggested. This process will activate spiritual power to work for you for your greatest good.

Dear Archangel Gabriel:

* Please can you help me to communicate my true heart-based feelings?

* Please can you help reveal to me my life purpose?

* Please can you help me in my writing career or speaking career?

* Please can you help me to break free of my addictions and temptations?

* Please can you help me to cleanse and purify my life to bring me harmony and order?

* Please can you help me to purify my mind and emotions of all negativity?

* Please can you help to keep my faith strong and to give me hope that I will conceive a child?

* Please can you help me to be disciplined in my actions?

* Please can you help me to heal my conscience of guilt?

* Please can you help me to have clarity about (name something specific)?

* Please can you help me to clear away (name something specific) that no longer serves me?

* Please can you help me to cleanse my aura of any absorbed negative energies?

Archangel Raphael

Archangel Raphael's name translates as "God heals," and he is known as the healer of healers. This beautiful Archangel's Archeia is Mother Mary, and together they serve on the fifth ray of God's Divine light, the emerald green ray, helping to shine the energy of God's healing light to the world. Mary is also known as "Queen of the Angels." They have legions of healing angels working with them on the green ray of healing light, and together they help send healing energies to areas of the Earth that are in need of assistance. Healing energy is always needed in areas of war and natural disasters, and we can ask God to send His healing angels to areas of the Earth in need of help.

On a more personal level, Archangel Raphael and Mary will direct healing energies to the sick and the suffering. They will send healing energies into hospitals, and will also work alongside medical professionals and healers to help empower their healing work with people. Archangel Raphael and Mary can help us learn the science of healing so that we can discover powerful insight and knowledge that can help us to heal and repair our health issues and the circumstances of our life. Healing students can study with this mighty Archangel during their nightly visits to the Archangel Raphael's and Mary's etheric retreat.

Archangel Raphael is also known as the patron of travelers. He was a guide to Tobias along his journey and helped keep him safe from harm. In great works of art, Archangel Raphael is often portrayed as carrying a walking stick, which symbolizes the staff of life. Archangel Raphael and Mary will help protect you along your own spiritual journey and your life travels.

The following questions are examples of what you can ask Archangel Raphael to help you with. Simply form a clear focused mental intention requesting his help, and be as specific as you can be with your request; or, use the questions suggested. This process will activate spiritual power to work for you for your greatest good.

Dear Archangel Raphael:

* Please can you help me to heal with (name something specific)?

* Please can you help to protect me on my journey?

* Please can you send healing energy to my loved ones?

* Please can you help me attract abundance in my life?

* Please can you help me to develop healing abilities?

* Please can you help me to find the truth in a certain situation?

* Please can you help me have a good vision of my future?

* Please can you surround me with your green, healing light?

Archangel Uriel

Archangel Uriel's name translates as "light of God," and he is known as the angel of peace and service. This glorious Archangel's Archeia is Aurora.

Together they serve on the sixth ray of God's Divine light, the purple and gold ray, helping to shine the energy of God's peace into the world. Archangel Uriel can help you discover the light of God within you so that you can develop your spiritual power to bring you a greater level of inner peace. Archangel Uriel and Aurora can also help you to see the light of God in others, even when they have let this light grow dim, so that you can respond to them in a peaceful and loving way. They teach that it is important to regain your inner peace as quickly as you can whenever you lose your balance. Your inner peace can be compromised whenever you are emotionally and mentally stressed and upset, and this will affect the light of God within you. The quicker you can regain your emotional and mental equilibrium, the quicker you will regain your inner peace. Archangel Uriel and Aurora can help us see the light at the end of a very long, dark tunnel.

This magnificent Archangel is full of God's wisdom, and he will share this wisdom to all those who are ready to spiritually progress so that they can also begin to shine their own light of peace to the world. Archangel Uriel can also help us rise above our problems and see them from a new perspective so that we are able to see the light. He can help us to develop our insight so that we begin to see all of life through a higher clarity of mind, at which point we can make our free-will choices in a more enlightened way.

The following questions are examples of what you can ask Archangel Uriel to help you with. Simply form a clear focused mental intention requesting his help, and be as specific as you can be with your request; or, use the questions suggested. This process will activate spiritual power to work for you for your greatest good.

Dear Archangel Uriel:

* Please can you help me find a peaceful solution to resolve my issue? (Be specific.)

* Please can you help me to increase my level of knowledge?

* Please can you help me to develop wisdom in my life?

* Please can you help me to find inner peace in my life?

* Please can you help me gain clarity and insight about (name something specific)?

* Please can you send your peace angels to specific areas of the planet?

* Please can you help me to dissolve my inner fears?

Archangel Zadkiel

Archangel Zadkiel's name translates as "righteousness of God," and he is known as the Archangel of God's mercy, freedom, and forgiveness. This powerful Archangel's Archeia is named Holy Amethyst, and together they serve on the seventh ray of God's Divine light, the violet ray, helping to shine the energy of God's mercy into the world. Archangel Zadkiel can help free your energy from any incurred karma that is interfering with your health and your life if you seek forgiveness and freedom. Archangel Zadkiel and Holy Amethyst can also help you in matters of forgiveness so that you can free your energy from the depths of pain that keep you in karmic ties to others.

This mighty Archangel is known as the angel of freedom, and he can help you free yourself from your negativity so that you can find joy. The powerful transmuting energy of the violet flame can help you heal your physical health issues, overcome addictions, alter destructive behavioral patterns and habits, and empower you with God's mercy and love.

The following questions are examples of what you can ask Archangel Zadkiel to help you with. Simply form a clear, focused mental intention requesting his help, and be as specific as you can be with your request; or, use the questions suggested. This process will activate spiritual power to work for you for your greatest good.

Dear Archangel Zadkiel:

 * Please can you help me to forgive myself for (name something specific)?

 * Please can you help me to forgive others who have hurt me?

 * Please can you help me to transmute all absorbed psychic stress?

 * Please can you help me to transmute my negative karma?

 * Please can you help me to overcome my addictions, destructive behaviors, and habits?
   (Be specific.)

 * Please can you help me to connect with my higher self?

 * Please can you help me to transmute my anger, fear, and worries?

 * Please can you help to free me from the pain of my past (name something specific)?

Archangel Etheric Retreats

Each of the Archangels has his own retreat within the etheric realm that you can visit during sleep or mediation. If you decide which mighty Archangel's retreat you would like to visit, you should form a mental intention before you go to sleep, stating your desire to do so. During sleep your spirit will leave your body for its nightly astral travels, when it will pay a visit to the specific Archangel's retreat you requested. The Archangel will then work on your energy field by giving you healing waves of light energies to help you with what you most need help with. You will also receive Divine instruction to help you gain the knowledge and insight you need to help you heal and to improve your life circumstances. The following information includes each Archangel's retreat and the help that is made available to you during your visit there.

> **Archangel Michael's retreat** is located in the etheric plane above Banff, Canada. You can visit his retreat to ask for help with spiritual or physical protection, courage, and inner strength to face things, and help in developing leadership qualities.

Archangel Jophiel's retreat is located in the etheric plane above the Great Wall of China. You can visit his retreat to receive wisdom and illumination.

Archangel Chamuel's retreat is located in the etheric plane above St. Louis, Missouri. You can visit his retreat for help with all matters of the heart.

Archangel Gabriel's retreat is located in the etheric plane above Mount Shasta, California. You can visit his retreat for help with purification of your energy vibration.

Archangel Raphael's retreat is located in the etheric plane above Fatima, Portugal. You can visit his retreat for help with healing and for Divine instruction about the science of healing.

Archangel Uriel's retreat is located in the etheric plane above Poland. You can visit his retreat for help with releasing your fears and igniting inner peace.

Archangel Zadkiel's retreat is located in the etheric plane above Cuba. You can visit his retreat for help with transmutation of negative energies and help with issues of forgiveness. The following meditation will help you to visit Archangel Zadkiel's retreat to receive help with issues of forgiveness so that you can gain freedom of spirit and find some inner peace.

Meditation Exercise:
Visiting Archangel Zadkiel's Retreat

* Use the white light of protection exercise. (See Chapter 2.)

* Close your eyes and settle yourself into a comfortable breathing rhythm. Begin by taking a few long and slow deep breaths in through your nose and out of your mouth; this will help to get the energy flowing in your body. When you breathe in, imagine the aura around you expanding, and when you breathe out, feel yourself relaxing more deeply. Do this several times.

* Open your chakras from the base to the crown by visualizing each one as spinning around in a clockwise direction (as if you were the face of the clock) and expanding. Use the color of each chakra to help you keep your focus strong: red, orange, yellow, green, turquoise blue, indigo, violet. You have now prepared your energy frequency.

✳ Set a mental intention that you would like to visit Archangel Zadkiel's etheric retreat. Let's begin!

✳ Ask your guardian angel to escort you to Archangel Zadkiel's etheric retreat. Feel the love of your guardian angel enfold you as you imagine taking its hand and leaving your body behind to go on your spiritual journey. You soon arrive at Archangel Zadkiel's retreat, which is located in the etheric realm over the island of Cuba, known as the temple of purification.

✳ This magnificent temple encompasses the violet flame, which can help you to accomplish forgiveness, transmutation, and freedom. You are taken to the place where the violet flame blazes, which is among many healing amethyst crystals. There you meet with the mighty and powerful Archangel Zadkiel, whose vibration radiates Divine love and compassion for you. Archangel Zadkiel is ready to take your hand and lead you into the center of the violet flame. Step into the center of the violet flame and feel it bathe your energy vibration with its healing power. Feel your energy immersed in the cleansing, healing vibration of the violet flame. You begin to feel cleaner, lighter, and freer.

❋ Ask Archangel Zadkiel to help you have the strength to forgive (say the person's name), or help you forgive yourself. Release all of your painful emotions into the flame of light, knowing that they will immediately dissolve. Once you have finished, step out of the flame, give thanks to Archangel Zadkiel, and take hold of your guardian angel's hand, ready to return back to your body.

❋ Now it's time to close down. Simply bring your awareness back into the room. Feel the weight of your body on your chair, move your fingers and toes, and open your eyes. Visualize intense white light pouring into your crown chakra and traveling through the central energy column until it reaches your base chakra. The white light will help to return your chakra frequencies back to their normal rates and sizes so that you will remain in a healthy, balanced state. Repeat the following affirmation: "I am grounded." Have a drink of water or a light snack to help ground your energy.

You can use this exercise whenever you feel any old emotions resurfacing. Your emotions can hold many different aspects of pain, depending on how deep the hurt is, and several healing journeys may be needed to help you release all related emotions.

You can visit any of the Archangels' retreats whenever you feel the need to. Soon enough, you will begin to feel happier and more fulfilled in your life.

———

My Angel Blessing to You

Many years ago I channeled a lovely message from the angels in the form of a poem with the intention of inspiring others toward healing themselves and their lives. It is my hope that this poem will help uplift and inspire you to remember all of the guidance that is made available to you by a higher power. Whenever you feel the need for support, you can read the poem and call on your angels, knowing that when you do, help is already being administered to you.

"Changes"

Our life is one of constant motion,
   forever changing like the ocean

Fearing the outcomes we cannot see, we
   stay where we are and constantly be

We stay in the pain of an old romance;
   we stay in the pain of not taking that
   chance

We stay in our grief of a love that has
    passed; not willing to move or let go of
    the past

We regret things we did or did not do;
    we hold onto anger and emotional
    blues

We blame other people and then
    ourselves, for the hurt and the upset
    and our poor health

When we feel we are ready for a new
    start, we gear ourselves up to play our
    part

But fear creeps in of "what if I fail?" I
    will be worse off than I am today

So maybe I will just sit on the fence, and
    wait till I get another chance

For staying, no movement, repeating the
    pain, will just hold you back again and
    again

Remaining in pain not living your truth,
    being stuck in your life being hurt and
    unsure

Not willing to change for fear of fear, not
    willing to move or progress any nearer

Can cause so much sadness and other
    ills, depression, headaches, and
    emotional hills

Not knowing what's wrong is sometimes right, to ask yourself this: "Am I happy in my life?"

For if the answer is no, then aspire to change — what is holding you back and then spread your wings

For freedom can come from the choices you make, the knowledge you learn the risks you take

When you make the first move you are starting to heal, your mind, your soul, and your body too

The spirit world applauds you through and through

Trust intuition no matter how hard

Know what you want, have faith in God

There is nothing you cannot cope with, with God on your side

He sends us His **Angels** to be by our side

For it takes courage to change and confidence too

Ask and receive the **Angelic Guidance** through

So the message here from the spirit world is;

Go for your dream no matter how small,
  do what you want and go for that goal

Live your truth and follow your heart,
  ask for assistance in order to start

Love yourself and love your life

Because with love in your soul; you will
  never, ever fail...

Author's Message

Know that you are being watched over by a higher power, as God, through His angels, is ready to work some wonder into your life. You have the aura power and potential you need to co-create the life you dream of, and to find some inner peace and fulfillment along the way. Now is the time to let your light shine....

Angel Blessings,
Joanne Brocas

Index

About the Author

JOANNE BROCAS offers angel workshops and healing workshops internationally that are fun, insightful, and energetically powerful. Joanne is the founder of Chakra Medicine School of Energy Healing & Intuitive Development, which offers certificated healing courses. You can find out further details about Joanne and her workshops and courses by visiting her Website: *www.chakramedicine.com*.